# TAEKWONDO

# TAEKWONDO

## Traditional Art & Modern Sport

## Eddie Ferrie

The Crowood Press

First published in 1989 by
The Crowood Press Ltd
Ramsbury, Marlborough
Wiltshire SN8 2HR

Paperback edition 1993
This impression 1999

British Library Cataloguing-in-Publication Data

A catalogue record for this book is
available from the British Library

   ISBN  1-85223-757-0

Dedicated to my wife Salud for all her constructive critism, endless patience
and loyal support.

Acknowledgements

This book could not have been written without the help and encouragement of
the following people. Firstly I am deeply indebted to Master Frank Massar, a
man I have come to know as a true martial artist of remarkable ability and a
good friend who made himself available for photo sessions and offered a host of
useful tips and information. Thanks also to the students at his Yin Yang
Taekwondo Academy for help with the photo sessions.

Thanks too to Phil Stone, David Mather and Geoff Bloomfield at GB
Photographic, as truly professional a pack of lensmen as exists anywhere, for all
their advice and instruction on the printing of photographs.

Finally thanks to Terence Donovan, Nicholas Soames and Katsuhiko
Kashiwazaki, without whom there would be no book.

Line illustrations by Ursula Matthews.

Typeset by Alacrity Phototypesetters,
Banwell Castle, Weston-super-Mare, North Somerset.
Printed in Great Britain by J W Arrowsmith Ltd, Bristol.

# Contents

# 1 History and Philosophy of Taekwondo

Taekwondo is an indigenous Korean martial art which has in the latter part of the twentieth century developed into a dynamic combat sport. It was the Seoul Olympic games that saw the introduction of taekwondo as a demonstration sport, and consequently it was shown to the world as a separate entity to the numerous forms of karate and kung fu with which it has for so long been confused, eventually becoming established world-wide as an independent modern combat sport in its own right. The modern Olympic version of taekwondo, however, is a direct development from the indigenous Korean forms which have existed for over two thousand years.

The word 'taekwondo' means 'hand and foot way' and this gives an indication of the nature of the activity, that is, as a combat sport in which hands and feet are used to defeat an opponent. Taekwondo is a fighting art similar in many ways to Japanese karate, but at the same time it is quite unique and distinct in its forms and techniques.

Despite a complex and highly developed point scoring system the main aim is, as in Western boxing, to knock out the opponent. The major difference is that it is not permissable in taekwondo to use punches to the head to achieve this end. The use of spectacular full-contact jumping and high-kicking techniques to score points and, if possible, to knock the opponent unconscious, is what distinguishes the Olympic version of the sport from related systems.

Taekwondo reflects the martial spirit of the Korean race, an iron-willed people always capable of defending themselves against aggression, from the ancient times of the three kingdoms to the modern Republic of Korea. This self-defence art was originally called Soobak, Kwonbaek, Byon, Tagyok or Taerkyon. It was only in the modern era that the name of taekwondo was adopted with the transformation of the self-defence system into a modern combat sport with diversified and systematised techniques. Taekwondo is unusual in that both attack and defence can be conducted from any direction: front, rear, right or left, using head, hands, feet, knees and elbows.

At taekwondo clubs trainees go through several stages of training, starting with mental discipline. This mental discipline is the fundamental basis for further training and without it the trainee will not progress very far. Following basic training on stance and guard, trainees study various movements including blocks, punches, strikes and kicks. As training progresses the patterns of stance become more diversified and complicated, allowing simultaneous execution of two movements or more from the same position. This develops speed, power and flexibility.

As well as offering a system of defence and counter-attack aimed at vital areas of the assailant's body, taekwondo offers direct and combination attack training, so that a skilled exponent can take the initiative if the situation requires it. If the basic movements are the ABC of taekwondo, the patterns are the

grammar of the system and any student hoping to progress has to master them, as well as the fighting techniques. Fighting ability is only one aspect of the art and alone will not allow a person to go all the way in taekwondo.

The Korean word for pattern, the equivalent to the *kata* in karate, is *poomse*. There are two groups of eight poomse which beginners have to practise and study: the *taegeuks* and the *palgwe* (sometimes written *palgyae*). The more recently evolved taegeuk group of patterns covers the same essential movements and principles and has virtually replaced the palgyae as the definitive core of study for trainees in the taekwondo system. The taegeuks take their name from the circles and bars of the Taeguggi symbols on Korea's national flag. Having mastered the basic patterns, trainees progress to the more advanced poomse: Koryo, Taebaek, Pyongwon, Shipjin, Phongwhon, Jitae, Hansoo and Ilyo.

There is a saying in taekwondo that 'Taekwondo begins and ends with civility'. This idea is central to the practice of all true martial arts. It is manifest in taekwondo as soon as a student enters the *dojang* (training hall) when he greets the instructor with a bow, to show courtesy and respect. The instructors reciprocate by bowing also. Once they have bowed all those in the dojang dedicate themselves wholeheartedly to their training. There is no secret to progress – all that is required is concentration, dedication and hard work. When the session ends, trainees and instructors bow to each other once again. This gives all training sessions a clear structure and direction and builds a system of discipline and control within which aggression can be harnessed and channelled constructively.

Before practising free sparring (*Kyorugi*), trainees gain skill in poomse and progress to patterned sparring in which they train by running through pre-set methods and tech-niques of attack and defence. Free sparring is the final phase of training prior to actual competition and can be practised with varying degrees of force. As an activity taekwondo is very demanding both mentally and physically and develops fitness, agility, balance and poise. The psychological benefits of practice outweigh even the considerable physical benefits. Students of taekwondo develop strength of character, a spirit of perseverance and self-denial which leads in turn to greater composure and confidence.

The ultimate purpose of taekwondo is to make a good human being. The strongly developed underlying moral precepts of tae-kwondo are an intrinsic part of the art and originate from centuries ago in the era when Korea suffered from internecine strife and was threatened by foreign invasion. A warrior caste – the Hwa-rang – grew out of the people's need for self-protection, and just as there was a code of chivalry among knights in Western Europe during the Middle Ages so there was among the Hwa-rang over a thousand years before.

# HISTORY AND ORIGINS

The first recorded communal life in Korea dates back to the era of the legendary founder of Old Korea, Tangun, who purportedly established the Korean nation in 2333 BC at Asdal. As in the histories of other nations, communal life gradually led to the formation of tribal societies and leagues and eventually took the form of a state. Historical records indicate that some 2,000 years ago in these tribal states there existed the custom of making offerings to heavenly deities with festivals of dance, music and games. The most important of these festivals were Yohgko of Puyo, Tongmaeng of Koguryo, Muchon of Yeh and Mahan and Kabi of Silla.

In the absence of any extant historical documentation the nature of the sports which existed at that time can only be guessed at. However, when the background of the age of hunting is taken into consideration it is obvious that there existed methods of preying as well as self-protection. The spear and the bow and arrow were among the tools of survival and were probably the subject of contests of skill. The evolution of hunter societies alongside agricultural communities saw the development of martial systems for attack and defence and it was within this framework that the earliest taekwondo techniques were developed. Some theorists point to wild animal attacks as a factor in the development of taekwondo, but the greatest threat to man has always been other men and the physical superiority of most animals is such that weaponless defence against them is hardly feasible. To put it another way, those animals which an unarmed man can defeat he can defeat without recourse to specialised taekwondo techniques. Animals like bears and lions on the other hand could not possibly be killed without the use of weaponry.

However, the common horse might help to explain the existence of certain taekwondo techniques, namely the high or flying kick. Such kicks evolved as battlefield weapons particularly in guerrilla campaigns against mounted enemies. Attacking an unsuspecting enemy on horseback by knocking him out of the saddle with a surprise flying kick was an entirely practical technique. This is especially true where a group of men on foot could surround a horse to prevent it moving and where it was possible to jump down at the enemy from a tree or from higher ground. Because of the ease of avoidance these flying kicks were almost certainly limited to ambush situations against a mounted enemy but could no doubt be very effective as a means of negating the horseman's superiority particularly on uneven terrain. Training to improve jumping and kicking power doubtless led to certain individuals being capable of unhorsing an enemy on level ground and the legacy of this skill can be seen in modern demonstrations of the awesome kicking abilities of many taekwondo experts.

# THE THREE KINGDOMS

The first nineteen monarchs of Koguryo ruled the kingdom from Tungko until the capital was moved to Pyongyang in AD 427. Although no existing historical records on Koguryo describe the cultural aspects of the kingdom, archaeological relics shed light on some of the manners and customs of the time. Among the sources of such relics are a number of tombs including the Muyong Chong tomb which contains a mural depicting two young men engaged in taekwondo sparring and a number of women performing a group dance. In the mural, the man on the left can be seen defending his mid-section with his left hand in a left forward stance, while the man on the right is about to attack with an open-handed strike, both nearly the same as movements found in modern taekwondo sparring.

A Japanese archaeologist who discovered and excavated the tomb said in his work *Study of Culture in Ancient Korea* that '... judging from the mural, the man to whom the tomb belonged must have been devoted to taekwondo in his lifetime hence a taekwondo scene was painted in his tomb to solace his spirit'. In as much as the date of the tomb was determined to be between AD 3 and AD 47, when the capital of Koguryo was in Tungko, it can be safely assumed that taekwondo was well known by then. The fact that a wealthy noble had his tomb decorated with a taekwondo mural also indicates that the warrior aristocracy as well as commoners used taekwondo to build up martial skills.

A similar scene was found in a painting in another Koguryo tomb of about the same time. In it, a man in a drill suit with a belt around the waist, strikingly similar to today's taekwondo training costume, is seen posing in a stance making a downward block with the left hand and an overhead block with the right hand. In view of this man's role as a guardian deity positioned in front of a tomb, just as in the case of 'Keumgang Yoska' in the later Silla era, it is apparent that taekwondo enjoyed popularity as a national art. Indeed there are theories amongst Korean archaeologists that the festivals of Yongko of Puyo and Muchon of Yeh and Mahan were ancient versions of taekwondo. If this assumption is correct then the first World Taekwondo Championships held in Seoul in May 1973 constituted belated recognition of an art established over two millenniums before.

Further historical evidence exists which makes it possible to trace the development of taekwondo throughout the history of Korea. The kingdom of Paekje, in the south-western part of the Korean peninsula, with its central zone around the Han river, was an area which traded extensively with China and Japan. The kings of Paekje were patrons of the martial arts and encouraged their people to engage in horseback riding, archery, taekwondo and Sirum (a type of wrestling) according to the ancient records. By the year 670 the dominant kingdom in Korea was that of Silla, which conquered Paekje in 668 and Koguryo in 670, effectively unifying the peninsula. The basis of Silla's military successes and her power was the unique warrior system of Hwa-rang do.

The Hwa-rang comprised youths of noble families devoted to the cultivation of mind and body which expressed the martial spirit of the nation and which became the root of national morality and strength. The Hwa-rang followed rigid commandments of loyalty to the king and were characterised by their filial piety, bravery in battle, trustworthiness to friends and prudence in taking life.

There is strong evidence to indicate that the Hwa-rang drilled in taekwondo. In front of the Sokkuram Grotto in Kyongju, which was built during the reign of King Kyongdok of Silla, stand two stone statues, the Keumgang Yoska, which clearly represent warriors in taekwondo stances which are employed in the modern pattern that takes its name from them: Keumgang.

Silla was superseded by the new dynasty of Koryo founded by Wangkon in AD 918. Koryo endeavoured, with some success, to expand its territory towards the north while effectively fending off external aggression. At this time taekwondo was known as Soobak and had reached a high level of popularity with detailed rules and thousands of practitioners. Soobak was taught to the armed forces and skilled exponents received rapid promotion through the ranks. Taekwondo exponents were afforded greater social rank and privileges on account of their abilities than at any prior time. General Chong Pu even made the practice of taekwondo compulsory for members of the army. King Ui Jong made his esteem for the art abundantly clear when he promoted Yi-Ui-Min, a noted exponent of it, from Taechong to Pyolchang (the equivalent of a modern Commander-in-Chief) on the basis of his taekwondo expertise. Annual tournaments were held from which the champions were selected to become high-ranking officials and even generals in the army! All of these facts are recorded in the official volumes entitled *The History of Koryo*.

The continued importance of taekwondo to the Korean nation is apparent from a variety of historical records. A war history written at the end of the sixteenth century describes how some seven hundred unarmed volunteer soldiers from the Kumsan area using only their bare hands (and feet) fought back the Japanese during the Hideoshi invasion. The Yi dynasty saw the writing of a unique martial arts book in 1790. The book, *Mooyedobotongji* by General Yi Dok-mu was commissioned at the command of King Chongjo and was a sort of military martial arts manual describing a variety of taekwondo techniques. The work was some forty pages long and contained drawings printed from carved wooden blocks.

# 2 Modern Taekwondo

## POLITICS OF THE SPORT

The history of modern taekwondo began in Korea on 19 September 1961 when the Korean Taekwondo Association was inaugurated. Soon after, it affiliated itself with the Korean Amateur Sports Association on 25 June 1962 and was admitted as an official event of the National Athletic Games for the first time at the 43rd National Games in October 1962.

The founder of modern taekwondo is generally regarded as being General Choi Hong Hi who was responsible for the founding of the International Taekwondo Federation (ITF). However, the ITF is not the body responsible for the inclusion of taekwondo in the Olympic games. The more recently formed (1973) World Taekwondo Federation (WTF) is the organisation which has been officially recognised by the International Olympic Committee (IOC) and only members of affiliated groups are eligible for selection for the Olympic games. The WTF was founded following the first World Taekwondo Championships which were held in 1973 at the Kukkikwon, the Korean Mecca of taekwondo, which was opened on 30 November 1972. Nineteen countries participated in these first world championships and since then the number has steadily increased. Korea took first place at the inaugural championships, the United States came second with China and Mexico taking the joint-third place. Following the success of the championships Dr Un Yong Kim, the head of the Korean Taekwondo Federation was elected to be the first president of the WTF.

## RULES AND ASSOCIATIONS IN GREAT BRITAIN

The official body for the sport affiliated to the WTF in Great Britain is the British Taekwondo Board of Control (BTBC). However there is a variety of other organisations practising various forms of taekwondo in Great Britain and throughout the world. The major difference separating many of these organisations is in the degree of contact which is allowed when the competitors fight.

The United Kingdom Taekwondo Association (UKTA) was originally the principal organisation in Great Britain but, for various reasons, many clubs and instructors broke away to form the Taekwondo Association of Great Britain (TAGB), which promotes the ITF semi-contact style of taekwondo. The United Kingdom Taekwondo Federation (UKTF) was likewise formed as a breakaway group from the UKTA because of basic philosophical and political differences and its members practise and compete in a system which devotes equal attention to patterns, breaking and light-contact sparring and which they feel is more suited to what their members want, making it more of a martial art than a contact sport. Another recently formed organisation is the British Taekwondo Federation (BTF), which is affiliated to the WTF and which has a number of members not happy with the way things were being done in the BTBC. They are a full-contact organisation and have many high standard fighters in their organisation. Confusion reigns politically speaking and this

Fig 1 WTF taekwondo is a full-contact sport in which the fighters wear headguards
and body armour.

will doubtless continue to be the case for some time.

The main point to bear in mind when considering taking up taekwondo is the nature of the martial art you want to practise. If you like full-contact and have Olympic aspirations you must practise WTF-style taekwondo and the BTCB is the association to join (although the future of taekwondo as an Olympic sport has yet to be assured). If you do not like the idea of full-contact and the inevitable injuries and painful conditioning training that are a part of the sport you may prefer semi-contact as practised by the TAGB, whose best fighters are technically excellent athletes who could doubtless do extremely well were they to compete in the full-contact area. The whole sporting aspect of taekwondo may be something you attach little importance to and you may be more concerned with practising and improving your health, fitness and ability to defend yourself, in which case there is no disadvantage in going to a UKTF or UKTA club. In the final analysis the best place to train is the best club in your area, which will normally be the one which has the best instructors and which does the most for its members. The best advice is to try them all, see what they offer and judge the situation for yourself.

## Rules

The rules of taekwondo are fairly straightforward and apart from differences in the degree of contact allowed are fairly universal. The target area for kicks and punches is from the waist to the top of the chest stopping at the collar bone, which means that the throat and neck are prohibited areas for attack.

*Fig 2   ITF-style taekwondo is semi-contact, but unlike WTF-style, fighters can score by punching to the head, so protective hand and footwear is normal kit.*

The back is also prohibited as a target area. In semi-contact taekwondo, points can be scored for punching attacks to the head, but in WTF-style taekwondo such attacks are completely forbidden. Sweeping or throwing the opponent to the floor are not allowed, and there is no ground fighting; combat only takes place with both fighters on their feet.

## Uniform

The equipment needed to begin practising taekwondo is fairly simple and inexpensive. The most crucial item is the taekwondo uniform, a loose-fitting cotton jacket and trousers tied in the middle with a belt, the colour of which denotes the grade of the person wearing it. The beginner's uniform is white, but when the grade of black belt is reached the exponent is entitled to wear a top with a black trim around the neck of the jacket. The top is different to the kind of jacket worn in karate, being a smock-like design rather than a jacket which might open and flap about in competition.

## Protective Equipment

Apart from the uniform the next really important piece of equipment, at least for male taekwondo practitioners, is a box. Because of the nature of the sport, involving fast kicking and lots of jumping and spinning with fighters often turning through 360 degrees to deliver blows, accuracy is not always possible to guarantee and the testicles need protection from accidental injury. The box ought to be of the type worn by boxers to protect against low blows, and can be worn on the outside of the trousers, as the cheap plastic cup type normally slipped inside the jockstrap can become displaced and trap the genitals which could lead to serious injury if a blow were to land there.

For serious competitors a dental gumshield is also an indispensable piece of equipment and it too should be of the individually moulded kind used by boxers. The other vital piece of protective equipment is a headguard, but this is generally only worn in actual competition or heavy sparring sessions. The main function of the headguard is to protect the skull from concussion should the fighter be knocked down by a kick.

As well as a headguard, taekwondo competitors should also wear body armour. This is very light, but allows full power kicks and punches to be unleashed against the body. Having said that, while competitions are always held in weight categories, in sparring it is quite common for fighters of differing weights to be paired together and the heavier fighter must obviously take care not to injure lighter training partners. The same is also true when highly experienced fighters are paired up with novices: no good instructor will countenance bullying in the dojang.

Less essential items include shin, instep and forearm pads, which can be used to help prevent bruising or to protect already bruised areas from further damage. Many fighters use padded sparring mitts for both hands and feet which obviously protect those areas of the body from injury but also reduce the risk of injury to the opponent or training partner.

## Appeal

People of both sexes and all ages practise taekwondo in one of its various forms and have found that it can be a really enjoyable activity. Although full-contact is not everyone's cup of tea, the art contains a variety of elements offering something for everyone. The flexibility exercises which are an integral part of warming up for training provide the body with an excellent series of stretches, as good as any yoga class, and the amount of moving and jumping about involved in a

Fig 3   The basic outfit for taekwondo practice and competition. Headguard, body armour and groin protector. The light cotton uniform should allow total freedom of movement. Instep and forearm protectors are optional extras.

session makes it a demanding activity from an aerobic point of view.

On the non-competitive side, taekwondo offers its students the chance to train in patterns (poomse) and self-defence techniques. In terms of exercise, practising poomse is like doing vigorous gymnastic dance and quite apart from anything else gives both men and women an excellent aerobic workout. Apropos of self-defence, taekwondo tends to be an eclectic system and it is continually being added to. Any effective unarmed method of fighting can have something to offer and taekwondo as an open-ended system is capable of incorporating any 'new' techniques into its repertoire although it remains almost exclusively a 'hard' martial art, relying on muscular generated force rather than on any of the internal forces (*chi* or *ki*) fundamental to many of the softer arts, which, with the exception of aikido, tend to be of Chinese origin.

## The Grading System

There are no short cuts to real mastery of taekwondo. There does exist, however, a system of stepping stones which help to keep the student motivated and provide him or her with short-term goals within training.

Competition is not for everyone, but as students progress in their training they are regularly graded. The idea of grading is very helpful and allows trainees to keep a check on their progress at the same time as it motivates them to improve. There are ten Kup grades in taekwondo, spread over five different coloured belts. These range, in ascending order, from 10th Kup (white belt) to 1st Kup (red belt with a black tab). The colour sequence goes; white, yellow, green, blue and red. A 10th Kup white belt and a 9th Kup white belt are distinguished by the fact that a 9th Kup will have a yellow tab on his belt, indicating that he is approaching the next

grade, which is that colour. This is true throughout the system, thus a 7th Kup will have a yellow belt with a green tab, a 5th Kup a green belt with a blue tab, a 3rd Kup a blue belt with a red tab and a 1st Kup a red belt with a black tab. The even number Kup grades will in each case have the corresponding plain belt without the tab. After reaching 1st Kup (red belt with a black tab) the trainee takes a Dan grading in order to wear the coveted black belt. The first black belt is called the 1st Dan grade, and after still further training it is possible to progress through the Dan grades where a higher number indicates a higher grade. International instructor grade is set at 4th Dan, which can only be awarded by a panel of 7th Dans. The highest grade possible is 9th Dan.

If a trainee does two sessions per week the normal time between gradings should be from three to four months, although of course it is possible to progress more rapidly if the trainee puts in the time and work. Dedicated, talented individuals can jump grades. The average time to reach black belt standard is about two and a half to three years although some people can get there sooner, while others never do. Once you have reached black belt the degree of difficulty of the gradings increases. There are also time limitations imposed – eighteen months must elapse before it is possible to be promoted to 2nd Dan and then a further two years before 3rd Dan. Of course to reach these exalted grades a lot of hard work has to be done, since it is not just a question of promotion for time served in the art!

The form of the grading normally involves performing basic techniques as well as poomse in front of an examiner or board of examiners who assess the students' competence. Ability in sparring has to be demonstrated also and some organisations require their members to be proficient at breaking. It is the examiners' decision as to whether or not to award the student a higher grade and if a sufficient level of improvement has not been shown his or her grade will remain the same. Students are not downgraded even if they have a particularly bad day when they grade. Once a grade is achieved it is for life.

The standards of grading vary considerably in different organisations so it is wise to bear in mind that a grade's meaning is defined by the system in which it is earned. Some styles of modern martial arts have evolved where the grading system is far removed from the traditional oriental concepts and as a consequence the grades of exponents within these systems are meaningless in any wider context. By traditional standards a thirty year old 10th Dan is an impossibility. In some cases these so-called masters award the grade to themselves. As a result it is possible to find individuals who purport to hold 8th, 9th and 10th Dans in esoteric martial systems who, if judged on their abilities, would quite often fail a 3rd Dan grading in the more rigorous traditional grading systems of reputable associations. To reach black belt standard in the Yin Yang Taekwondo Academy under Master Frank Massar for instance, takes a minimum of five years, but as a consequence his dojang has produced a number of WTF-style national champions, who although still only red belts have beaten 2nd and 3rd Dans of other associations.

The important thing about grading is not to be in a hurry. It is also worth considering the notion that an extremely high grade does not necessarily mean an individual will make a good instructor. The eager student is only really limited by the distance he or she is willing to travel to train with the best instructor. It is worth looking around and trying a few different sessions to find the right environment for your own training. Some people have joined clubs in the hope of being taught by a 9th Dan only to find that the 9th Dan is so busy with other things that he rarely has time to teach and they actually end up learning from a 1st Dan.

Before joining a club, check it out and make sure that it is affiliated to the MAC (Martial Arts Commission). If it is, it will be the genuine article. Having found the right club, the right instructor and the right association for your personality the rest is up to you. In the final analysis your progress in the art depends on your own efforts. A good instructor can guide you in the right direction and speed up your progress, but ultimately you will have to sweat and strain and push yourself through arduous and demanding training sessions to reach your goal. If you work very hard and retain your enthusiasm and willingness to learn, especially when you reach the Dan grades, there is no reason for not fulfilling your potential. The key to progress in taekwondo as in everything else in life is dedication to what you are doing. This may seem a daunting prospect considering that many of the more serious practitioners of the art are so hooked by what they are doing that they are hardly conscious of the degree of their own commitment, but on the positive side the activity does provide them with enormous self-satisfaction and a lot of fun along the way!

# 3 Stances and Steps

The idea of a fighting stance is central to most martial arts, but is widely misunderstood by many practitioners. The stance is the basis from which any technique proceeds. Taekwondo exponents systematically train in developing the ability to move fast in and out of stances, which in itself trains the muscles of the legs and improves speed and agility, but more importantly aids in making smooth transitions from one technique to the next, making the possibility of flowing combination techniques a reality. Practising the basic stances until the muscles of the legs quiver may be monotonous but it is a tried and tested method of developing power in many martial arts. It is a curious fact that the average beginner invariably finds it difficult to bend the knees and use the legs effectively especially when punching and, to a lesser extent, when kicking. This difficulty vanishes as the trainee makes progress through practising techniques with attention to stance.

Training with attention to stance is a conscious attempt to correct inefficient biomechanical actions, but when actually fighting the stances are only visible for split seconds as fighters flow from one technique to another – they do not move around 'in a stance', but adopt the required stance as and when it is necessary to effect techniques. The straddle stance for instance may seem irrelelevant to the beginner but after a year or two's training he or she will soon realise its value for recovering from kicking attacks which the opponent manages to avoid, for cross stepping in order to close distance, to permit an effective side kick and a host of other things.

## The Attention Stance *(Fig 4)*

The first stance any taekwondo exponent learns to adopt is the attention stance. This is not a fighting posture as such, but is adopted by students for standing and listening to their instructors prior to bowing either in competition or in practice. It is in this stance that taekwondo students learn to bow to training partners, teachers and ultimately their opponents. As can be seen from Fig 4 the hands are held by the sides, the heels are kept together and you always keep the eyes open and fixed on the opponent, although it is considered a sign of respect by many to lower the eyes when bowing to master instructors.

## The Ready Stance *(Fig 5)*

The ready stance is a relaxed, upright posture which is adopted after bowing either in poomse training or in competition and prior to any final bow. It is a natural posture from which the trainee can smoothly explode into action and is most useful for training the reflexes so that defensive measures can be readily adopted in self-defence situations before any blow is struck. In pre-arranged sparring the defender begins in this stance before initiating defensive movements, which helps train the reflexes against sudden attack.

## The Basic Forward Stance *(Fig 6)*

The basic forward stance is part of the core of taekwondo. The left stance is adopted from the ready stance position by stepping forward on the left foot and straightening the

Fig 4   *The standing bow (attention stance).*

Fig 5   The ready stance.

*Fig 6    The forward stance.*

right leg. The front (left) foot should be pointing straight forwards and the leg should be firmly bent. The back leg should be locked straight at the knee and the weight evenly distributed over both legs. The rear foot should be turned out at about forty-five degrees to the front foot. The left hand should be held about nine inches above the knee and the right hand pulled back into the hip, roughly on a line with the belt, palm turned upwards. Both hands should be correctly formed into fists, the front hand ready to block and the back to counter-punch. From the ready stance the trainee learns to move

forwards and backwards, to punch, to block and to kick. The stance is very stable in a forwards–backwards direction but does not have great lateral stability. This is the basic stance from which the host of movements that comprise taekwondo begin to be understood. It is the stance all beginners have to come to know and in which much of the pre-arranged sparring is practised.

## The Free Fighting Stance *(Fig 7)*

The free fighting stance is the stance most readily adopted for free sparring and occurs frequently in actual competition. The front foot points straight ahead and the back foot is at a right angle. The body-weight is fairly evenly distributed over the feet perhaps in a ratio of sixty to forty, but this is variable. Fighters who prefer to kick off their front foot will carry more weight on the back leg while those who prefer to land heavy kicks off the back leg will keep their weight more over their front leg. This is very much a question of personal preference and which techniques the fighting style of the opposition leaves open. The important thing to remember about the hands is to keep them up and away from the body. Many styles of karate have a similar free fighting stance but as the rules they fight under are very different they do not have to contend with full power jumping reverse turning kicks and axe kicks which simply smash a tight guard into the person trying to block, so they tend to bend the elbows more. Keeping the front hand well out in front is especially important as it allows the taekwondo exponent to feel the range from which an opponent fires his techniques.

## The Back Stance *(Fig 8)*

The back stance is one which can be easily adopted from the forward stance by simply

*Fig 7   The free fighting stance.*

*Fig 8   The back stance.*

## The Crane Stance *(Fig 9)*

The crane stance is a further progression from the tiger stance with the front foot actually lifted clear of the floor. It is a stance which offers a means by which to deal with footsweep attacks by lifting the attacked foot clear for a split second before using a kick as a counter-attack. It is probably the most difficult of the stances to hold for any length of time and is a good way of developing leg strength and balance simultaneously. It is important to practise this stance on the leg you prefer to actually kick with as well as your favoured supporting leg as this helps achieve symmetrical physical development. The stance takes its name from the fish-eating bird, the crane, which waits balanced on one leg before grasping its prey with a sudden combined beak and talon attack.

## The Straddle Stance *(Fig 10)*

Known as the horse stance by many other martial artists, the straddle stance is a fundamental posture which is crucial to developing the ability to move fast laterally. The weight is equally distributed over both feet which are kept slightly wider than shoulder width. The toes of both feet point straight forwards and the knees are bent. The beginner invariably has difficulty with this stance as there is an irresistible tendency to bend slightly at the waist and stick the backside out. This has to be avoided and is best achieved by keeping a straight back and developing strong leg muscles. The stance is frequently used for practising punches because thinking about the punching action helps trainees forget the agony of burning leg muscles as the exertion of maintaining the stance bites. However, the main use for the stance in combat is when using side kicks as it allows a laterally-facing opponent to move very smoothly and employ these techniques most effectively.

pushing the front leg straight and drawing the front foot back, transferring the weight on to the rear leg. It is a stance most beginners find quite difficult, the front leg being much closer to the rear than in the free fighting stance and almost all the weight being held upon the rear leg. The front leg is bent with only the toes and the ball of the foot on the floor and supports hardly any weight at all. The tiger stance is a form of modified back stance where the front foot is drawn closer still to the rear foot and is a stance from which a fighter can spring forwards into the attack, like a leaping tiger.

Fig 9   *The crane stance.*

Fig 10   *The straddle stance.*

Figs 11–13   *The cross step and double downward block.*

Fig 12

Fig 13

When moving laterally it is necessary to cross step to generate sufficient power to make kicks count. The cross step can be either in front or behind the supporting leg. In Figs 11–13 illustrating these steps a double downward block is also performed.

# 4 Striking Techniques

It is possible to make any strike or kick from a stationary position, but of course by moving the body greater force is generated. The great problem with any fighting system is that there always has to be a compromise between speed and power. Much has been written of focus and the importance of concentrating energy into a single spot as a blow is delivered, but the big problem in actual combat with skilled opposition is that the target is always moving. If a fighter attacks with a full power technique which his opponent is able to avoid, the kinetic energy released has to go somewhere. The attacker can either pull the technique back or in some cases change it into something else as when a crescent kick becomes a step into a reverse crescent kick. Indeed against a retreating opponent the ability to chase and put together combinations must be developed as this can be the deciding factor in winning a contest. However, the fighter who chooses to throw full power, full focus techniques is likely to burn up energy at a tremendous rate and tire rapidly, especially if the techniques do not connect. Also a combination out of a missed full power technique will not be as fast as a pre-planned combination where the first technique is deliberately employed to set up a second or third.

The key to power is to express strength as speed and the key to speed is relaxation. When studying technique therefore, the main priority is to relax and develop co-ordinated movements. In a sport where the opposition is difficult to hit it is more important to be able to hit quite hard often than very hard occasionally.

An important aspect of focus is the size of the striking area which transmits the force of the technique into the target. The two large knuckles of the index and middle finger are a more concentrated striking area than the whole of the hand, and the heel or the ball of the foot make better weapons than the entire sole or instep. The underlying ethos of taekwondo is that of obtaining maximum effect from minimum use of force. Put simply, a taekwondo strike sees the energy of an attack focused into a small, hard area which then collides at high speed with a vulnerable part of the opponent's body. Conditioning of hands and feet is an important consideration in taekwondo as it protects the striker from injury should he come into contact with a hard part of the opponent's body, such as the top of the head.

## PUNCHES

The two most basic punches in taekwondo are the stepping punch and the reverse punch; one embodies the attacking spirit and the other the defensive counter-attack.

## The Stepping Punch *(Figs 14–16)*

This is the basic technique used to train beginners to move the body as a unit. From left forward stance step forwards with your right leg, keeping the left knee bent as you do so. Raise your left hand to chest height and as your right knee comes through, punch simultaneously as you step on to your right foot. The punch should land in the same split second as the foot touches ground. As your right foot goes forward and you punch out with your right hand, pull your left hand back into your hip quickly. This increases the force of the punch and also leaves you instantaneously ready to deliver another punch with your left hand. The action of the hands is very important throughout the technique. When you begin the right fist is palm up, but as you punch at the last moment you twist your hand so that the punch lands in the palm down position. The previously outstretched hand does exactly the opposite and is drawn back to the hip with palm turning up at the last moment. The turning action of the fist is very important as it greatly increases the force of the blow on impact. The height of the head should be maintained level throughout the step, rather than bobbing up and down. The front leg should pull the hips through as the rear leg drives in order to increase the speed of the step.

Training for the stepping punch involves repeatedly doing the technique up and down the dojang. Practical considerations make it important to be able to turn around when doing this drill and of course the method for turning can be applied to make fast, sudden changes of direction when doing other techniques equally simple. The turn is normally performed as demonstrated in Figs 17–20 when the trainee reaches the end of the dojang. The last stepping punch that available space permits is executed, then the back foot moves across and the hips begin to turn. Spinning on the balls of the feet, both hands are lifted across the chest and cross in readiness to perform a downward block. The trainee completes the turn with the downward block, pulling the right hand back on to the hip in readiness to make further stepping punch movements.

Figs 14–16   *The stepping punch.*

Fig 15

Fig 16

Figs 17–20   The turning block.

Fig 18

Fig 19

Fig 20

## The Reverse Punch *(Figs 21–5)*

This is generally considered to be the bedrock technique in most styles of karate. In World Union of Karate Organisations (WUKO) karate in particular top competitions seem to be a duel between two people who use few other techniques. The first to land a reverse punch wins the point. The effectiveness of the technique is undeniable but its popularity is out of proportion in some styles as a consequence of the rules under which they fight, and this has led to a reduction of the art to an exchange of reverse punches, not very spectacular nor exciting for the spectator. The reverse punch, while an important technique to study for self-defence and contest in tae-kwondo, is nothing like the dominant technique of the system that it is in many other martial arts.

The reverse punch is generally performed either from the forward or free fighting stance. It is also very effective as a combination technique with other punches and kicks. The mechanics of the punch are very simple and it is especially useful for stopping an opponent who comes charging in, since it enables you to get your weight over your front leg and really lean into the technique as you feel it connect.

Figs 21–2   *The reverse punch (side view).*

Fig 22

Fig 23   *The reverse punch (front view).*

Figs 24–5   *The reverse punch is a very effective counter-punch as the opponent comes in. In full-contact it is advisable to get the body behind the punch and lean into it with the shoulder.*

Fig 25

# The Back Fist

This is a very useful technique from both the self-defence and semi-contact contest points of view. It is an extremely fast technique which beginners pick up quickly as it is relatively easy to perform and has a variety of applications, although the target area is almost invariably the face, which effectively rules it out of WTF-style full-contact. For the purpose of self-defence, the main target areas are the nose, temple and the side of the jaw. In semi-contact matches it is best to aim for the cheek as contact with the nose is likely to cause bleeding and the temple is a potentially lethal place to hit anyone. In traditional pre-arranged sparring there are two basic methods of striking with the back fist, the vertical and the horizontal.

## *The Vertical Back Fist* (Figs 26–8)

The vertical back fist is used to directly attack the face in a frontal manner. The nose is generally the best target with this technique which can have a sickening effect on any would-be assailant. The person hit with a back fist to the nose often has trouble seeing as a result, since the eyes tend to water when the nose is hit. The technique illustrated in Figs 26–8 demonstrates the direct attack with the vertical back fist from a back stance. The fighter in white is in the left fighting stance and his opponent is in the right back stance. Transferring his weight on to his front foot, the fighter on the right makes a half step to come into range, lifting and crossing his arms as he does so. He pulls his arms apart and re-assumes the back stance as he delivers the back fist. This is a forceful technique, not just a flick of the wrist. Note how the left fist is pulled down on to the hip as the right fist rotates and hits the target, magnifying the force of the blow.

Figs 26–8   *The vertical back fist as a direct attack.*

Fig 27

*Fig 28*

## The Horizontal Back Fist (Figs 29–31)

The horizontal or side back fist is used either like a jab, to draw an opponent's defence, or as a counter-attack. As with the vertical back fist, the target area is usually the face. The eyes, nose, cheek or jaw are all on offer against the side back fist in a self-defence situation although in sparring or semi-contact the cheek or side of the jaw is the only really acceptable target. It is also useful as a distraction technique to take the opponent's (or assailant's) attention away from a more powerful major technique such as a reverse punch or back kick.

A basic application of the technique is demonstrated in Figs 29–31 with the counter against a lunge punch. The attacker is in the left fighting stance and the defender is in the right fighting stance. As the attacker makes a lunge-punch attack the defender side-steps into a back stance, deflecting the punch with a knife-hand block and lifting his right fist to his left shoulder. He then steps into his attacker with the back fist aimed at the nose. Note the use of the blocking hand to grab the wrist and pull the opponent on to the technique, increasing the impact and making it more effective at the same time as the attacking hand is trapped and rendered ineffective.

Figs 29–31   *The horizontal or side back fist as a counter to a lunge punch.*

Fig 30

Fig 31

## Double Back Fist *(Figs 32-5)*

One particularly effective variant of the back fist technique which is used by many free-style martial artists is the double or spinning back fist. It is difficult to be accurate with this technique, but when it scores in semi-contact or free-style kick-boxing where it is permitted, it can be spectacular. It is shown in Figs 32-5 as a counter technique to a jab. As the attacker jabs, the defender side-steps and makes a twisting block with the left hand simultaneously whipping out a side back fist to the attacker's nose. Without pausing, he then rotates his upper body and spins on the balls of his feet from a right stance into a left back stance keeping both hands high to add momentum and speed to the spinning technique and to protect against counter-attacks to his own head. The second back fist hits with more force than the first and in many cases actually knocks out the opponent. Sometimes this technique is used in direct attack, often with the first back fist not actually hitting the target but causing the opponent to move his head, setting himself up for the effective completion of the spinning technique.

Figs 32-5    The double or spinning back fist combination.    Fig 33

Fig 34

Fig 35

42

# The Palm Heel *(Figs 36–8)*

The palm heel is a traditional technique which is studied mainly for self-defence purposes and is not used in competition. The main target areas for this technique are the jaw and the bridge of the nose. It can be particularly useful for those whose hands are not conditioned or who have stress fracture type injuries to the hands. It is often taught on self-defence courses to those women who find making a fist awkward. It does allow a blow to be delivered just under the nose without exposing the hands to the danger of damage from the assailant's teeth which can occur if a fist is used. In the example shown in Figs 36–8 of an application of the palm heel strike the attacker attempts a hooking punch which is blocked by a reverse knife-hand block. Note how the defender switches from back stance to reverse-punch posture to deliver the blow with the full force of his legs and hips, but maintains contact with his blocking hand rather than pulling back to the hips and leaving his head unprotected against a possible second attack.

Figs 36–8   The palm heel strike.

Fig 37

Fig 38

## The Knife-Hand Block *(Figs 39–41)*

The knife-hand is perhaps better known as the infamous karate chop, so publicised by James Bond films and sixties television series such as *The Avengers*. It is a very useful technique for self-defence purposes but requires considerable conditioning of the muscles of the hands in order to be really effective. Although permissible as a blocking technique it is not allowed in competition as an attack. It is typically demonstrated in breaking for which it is well-suited, allowing a great deal of force to be focused into a small surface area. There are many blocks and strikes which employ the knife-hand in taekwondo.

Figs 39–41 show a knife-hand block and grab followed by a knife-hand to the side of the neck. The soft parts of the body – the neck in particular – are natural targets for this technique but are very vulnerable and ought only to be attacked in self-defence in drastic circumstances. The fighter in black steps back from a left stance into a right stance as his assailant launches a reverse punch. He makes a knife-hand block with his right hand and quickly grabs his attacker's wrist. He then makes a small step to his rear on his right foot, lifting his left hand across and in front of him until it is almost level with his right ear. Having created enough space to step in with his left foot he pulls himself in on his attacker's wrist and strikes to his neck with a powerful assisted reverse knife hand.

Figs 39–41   *The reverse knife-hand block and reverse knife-hand strike, used to counter a reverse punch attack.*

Fig 40

Fig 41

45

## Elbow Strikes *(Figs 42–7)*

The elbows are among the most useful and powerful of taekwondo weapons when used in self-defence circumstances. The power of elbow strikes has frequently been witnessed in breaking competitions and demonstrations, but it is not allowed in competition under semi-contact or WTF rules. The only sport which does permit the use of elbow strikes to the head is Muay Thai kick-boxing as practised in Thailand. The three basic forms of the elbow strike are the upper-cut, smash and reverse elbow. Elbow strikes to the head must be considered as potentially lethal techniques, the reverse elbow to the temple being perhaps the most lethal as a great deal of force is concentrated into a small and very vulnerable area.

### *The Basic Elbow Strike* *(Fig 42)*

The basic elbow strike utilises the point of the elbow and is superbly effective when fighting close. The chin or the side of the jaw are ideal target areas for this technique. It is such a powerful technique that, for example, when it is done correctly, even a physically much weaker woman can knock out a male assailant.

Fig 42   *The basic elbow strike is an exceptionally powerful technique and very suitable for in-fighting.*

## The Upper-Cut Elbow Strike
### (Figs 43–4)

The upper-cut variant of the elbow strike is another devastating technique. In the example shown an inside block is used against a hook punch and the technique is applied at very close range. Note the same stance as is used for the reverse punch is applied in order to generate maximum force, with the upper body rotating fully, the hips turning square-on and the legs driving home the strike. As in the preceding technique, the jaw is the ideal target area for this strike.

*Figs 43–4  The rising upper-cut strike using the elbow.*    *Fig 44*

## The Spinning Back Elbow Strike
(Figs 45–7)

A more advanced technique utilising the elbow strike is the spinning back elbow. As demonstrated in the photographic sequence, the defender utilises an arm lock to prevent his attacker from avoiding the strike. This is a technique which requires split second timing and co-ordination, but is extremely effective. As the attacker makes a lunge-punch attack the defender springs into the back stance and makes a right inside block. He then loops his right hand over his attacker's outstretched arm and spins through 180 degrees, pivoting on his right foot and stepping behind on his left, lifting his elbow up as he does so. The attacker's arm is painfully locked at the elbow preventing him from escaping and he is unable to block the incoming elbow strike, even if he is aware of it. The defender delivers the blow from a strong straddle stance for maximum power and strikes the attacker's skull at the base of the ear.

Figs 45–7  *The armlock and reverse elbow strike.*

Fig 46

Fig 47

# 5 Blocks

Any discussion of the blocking techniques of taekwondo has to recognise that there are two distinct sets of circumstances in which a trainee will be required to produce an effective block. One set will be sports based, where the opponent will be using taekwondo techniques either in sparring or contest to score points. The other will be a self-defence situation where an assailant will be trying to inflict damage. The types of blocking technique required in such different circumstances may vary considerably.

The blocking techniques of taekwondo will be familiar to anyone who has studied karate. The inner and outer blocks across the front of the body protect the mid-section and lower face. The downward block protects the groin and lower abdomen. The rising head block protects the head and upper chest area. The blocks performed in the various poomse are designed for dealing with punching and kicking attacks. These conventional blocking techniques need to be considerably modified for contest as a result of the enormous power generated by the various kicking techniques when performed by experts. As well as being able to impact block by matching force for force in the traditional hard style martial arts, it is necessary to be able to deflect and also smother techniques.

The guard in taekwondo is normally characterised by the hands being held well up and away from the body. This allows the taekwondo exponent to keep out of range and to deflect or push off powerful kicks rather than attempting to stand still and absorb them. An axe kick or a jumping reverse turning kick will smash the blocker's hands into his or her own face or body if an attempt is made to adopt a solid, static defensive stance. The tight guard favoured by boxers and some karate fighters, where the main concern is blocking punches to the face, does not allow sufficient space for techniques such as the axe kick to be effectively stopped. Even taking such a kick on the arms, the force will be transmitted into the body and at the very least will have a staggering or balance-breaking effect. Defence against such powerful kicks has to be based upon movement. Only the strongest of martial artists can meet such attacks head-on. Rather than doing a rising block and hoping for the best, make the block and move out of the way by pushing yourself off the kicking leg.

The important thing to stress when using your arms to block a kick, particularly one that is coming crashing down on you with your opponent's full weight behind it, is that evasion is always better than opposition and blocks should deflect or smother attacks not attempt to break them as some hard styles of karate emphasise. Legs are stronger than arms. Get out of the way.

## Types of Block

There are many ways to block including closed fist, knife-hand, reverse knife-hand, open palm, forearms, elbows, knees and even shins. Points of contact when blocking are variable. Some masters emphasise blocking with the forearms which grow tougher through conditioning practice; others, aware that an opponent will have tough forearms, will suggest wrist to wrist and still others will

recommend using the hammer fist. For blocking some of the more powerful kicks, elbows and forearms can be used as can shins and knees. Leg blocks usually work well as a method of stifling kicks rather than as impact blocks. All are valid and viable methods in free fighting or sparring.

## The Downward Block *(Fig 48)*

The downward block is a powerful blocking movement generally delivered in the forward stance. The blocking hand, in this case the left, is normally lifted across the upper body to the opposite ear and from there it snaps down forcefully, the fist twisting at the last moment as it meets the incoming attack. The last-second twist is just as important in blocking as it is in punching and deflects an incoming fist or foot very successfully. This is an effective technique against stepping or reverse punches and also front kicks.

## The Rising Block *(Fig 49)*

The rising block is particularly useful against certain high kicks and any punches aimed at the face. The blocking action needs to be light and fast, the block being punched into position rather than simply placed there. From the ready stance the trainee can practise this block by stepping either forwards or backwards into the forward stance, lifting and crossing his arms at chest height then punching the blocking arm into place and twisting the forearm so that the palm faces outwards as he does so. The non-blocking arm is pulled in to the hip when punching to strengthen the block by virtue of the recoil effect and also so that the fighter is ready to launch a counter-attack.

Fig 49   The rising block.

Fig 48   The downward block.

## The Inner Block (Fig 50)

The inner block is a deflection block used mainly against punches to the face and body performed in the forward stance, the back stance or the free fighting stance. As the attacker punches, the defender deflects the punch inwards, striking the outside edge of the attacker's wrist with the little finger edge of his own wrist. Although the block can be performed from a static position it is made more powerful by stepping into it. The non-blocking arm is pulled to the hip in readiness for a counter-attack as the block is made. Fig 50 shows a left-handed inner block performed as the defender moves away from the attacker's reverse punch, out of a right forward stance and into a left back stance. Even executed whilst moving backwards the technique generates considerable force as withdrawing the right hip adds power to the inward twist of the waist transmitted through the shoulders and returns the attacking initiative to the defender. Unlike most of the other blocks described here this block does not originate from crossing raised arms and then pulling them apart. The blocking hand is instead raised level with the ear on the same side of the body as the arm being used to block with, and brought down and inwards, twisting as it lands.

## The Outer Block (Fig 51)

The outer block is less powerful than the inner block but is worthy of serious study all the same as it is particularly useful for competition. Like the rising block, it has the advantage of opening up the attacker's body, which is a relatively easy target, to major scoring techniques. Bear in mind that once a block is made it prevents the attacker using the arm which has been blocked for blocking any counter-attack. To perform the block as shown in Fig 51, step back from the left forward stance into the back stance, cross your arms left over right in front of your body as you retreat. The blocking arm, in this case the left, is held only slightly bent and pointing down to the floor while the right arm is bent, covering the chest, with the right fist almost touching the left shoulder.

Fig 51   The outer block.

Fig 50   The inner block.

## The 'X' Block *(Figs 52 and 53)*

The 'X' block employs the inside edges of both wrists to form a trap for punching or kicking attacks. Both arms are crossed in front of the chest and driven up or down as required to stop the incoming technique. Normally it is used to stop front kicks to the groin in self-defence situations where it is often followed up by a leg sweep. Its effectiveness in competition is limited though. The block is very powerful but totally commits the user, making it easy for the attacker to exploit the inherent weaknesses of the technique. When blocking the front kick, for example, the defender leaves the face and chest unprotected against punches and, conversely, when defending against head height punches the body is left wide open to kicking attacks. Of course, if the defender is much faster and more experienced than the attacker it is an effective block. The danger of over-committing oneself with this block is clearly illustrated in Fig 53 which shows a front kick scoring. After employing a feint front kick to

Fig 53   *By using a feint to draw the defender into committing himself to an 'X'-block, the attacker is able to kick over the block with a powerful front kick and score.*

Fig 52   *The 'X'-block, an effective block against an attempted kick to the groin.*

draw the defender into using the 'X' block, the kicker simply lifts his knee higher and slams home the kick over the block.

Other blocking techniques using the hands include knife-hand blocks and reverse knife-hand blocks *(see* Figs 36–41). Trapping blocks such as the one used in the reverse elbow strike technique are also popular in traditional one-step sparring where the trainee in the attacking role announces his or her intention to attack and the defender practises predetermined counters. The light, fast blocks required for competition differ considerably from the traditional forms but they are nevertheless effective if they prevent the attacker from connecting. The only really

viable alternatives to blocking are to duck, to take the kicks on the forearms, or to implement the old philosophy that attack is the best form of defence and take the fight to your opponent.

Fig 54 *Sometimes the best defence is evasion. Anyone learning taekwondo has to learn how to duck!*

Figs 55–6 *Children blocking effectively in competition.*

Fig 56

Figs 57–8 *ITF-style fighters in competition using their forearms to block kicks.*

Fig 58

# 6 Kicks

The kicking techniques of taekwondo are among the most varied and impressively spectacular of any in the martial arts. A large proportion of the training time of any taekwondo exponent is spent on developing these fast, accurate and powerful kicks. Because of the potentially hazardous nature of full-contact taekwondo a high level of fitness is one of the qualities that has to be developed before entertaining any thought of entering competition. This applies almost equally to semi-contact, for although the danger of actually being knocked out is a lot less, it still happens. Legs are approximately four times as strong as arms so the force that a trained expert can generate with a kick is enormous and fighting when not in good condition is potentially very dangerous. As well as good endurance, taekwondo fighters need to develop spring in the legs and a tough well-conditioned mid-section so that they can keep kicking and shrug off the punishment inflicted by their opponents.

A distinction needs to be made between the kind of techniques which are practical and advisable from a self-defence point of view and those which are primarily relevant to a competition situation. An expert could probably knock out most assailants with whatever technique he chose to employ but the majority of taekwondo practitioners need to be more down to earth. A jumping reverse crescent kick may well be a spectacularly decisive technique in a competitive situation but it would be very unusual for it to be used for the purpose of self-defence.

The head is frequently the target of taekwondo kicking techniques, so good range of movement and flexibility is very important. Even more important is the speed of delivery and accuracy of the kick. The focus of the technique must be concentrated upon the smallest possible area so the various kicks all have different striking areas. The front kick and turning kick are usually delivered with the instep or the ball of the foot. The side kick focuses its power into the side edge or heel of the foot and back kicks use the heel. Most kicks are delivered on the move in a taekwondo bout as the fighters are rarely static. A static target or one moving in a straight line, such as a would-be assailant about to wade in, is of course easier to hit and simple direct techniques can be employed. In competitive taekwondo it is much more difficult to hit opponents because their movements are so much harder to predict. The best fighters move forwards, backwards and laterally, throwing numerous feints and range-finding techniques to set up their opponents for major attacks. Mobility and the ability to use either leg are vital components of the successful competitor.

The ability to kick with both legs is extremely desirable in order to be able to set up the kind of combination attacks which will actually score in the heat of battle against a well-trained opponent. Top fighters throw as many kicks as boxers do punches in the course of competition and in order to score these need to be just as fast and accurate and even more elaborate in their use of feints and combinations. This is tremendously tiring and demands superb fitness and conditioning as well as the ability to absorb punishment during the course of a match.

# TYPES OF KICK

## The Front Kick *(Figs 59–63)*

The most basic kicking technique in tae-kwondo is the front kick which can be delivered off the front or the back leg. The front kick can be a pushing kick aimed at creating sufficient space to facilitate a follow-up with another technique such as a turning kick, or it can be a thrusting kick intended to hurt the opponent. In a self-defence context it can also be effective as a snap kick.

The front kick is generally one of the first kicks to be taught in taekwondo, and this teaching differs slightly from the methods stressed in Japanese karate, where the student has to develop a low, powerful stance from which to perform his techniques with the conviction that each and every one will end the contest. The taekwondo student on the other hand is taught to kick rapidly and repeatedly from a moving posture as fighters in competition rarely stand still and a single kick only occasionally ends such a match.

The power and speed of the kick carried out on the move can be much greater than that delivered from a fixed stance, provided that the moving body-weight of the kicker is transmitted through it. In addition, students learn right from the beginning to cover ground and reach their opponent with the technique, which is often the most

*Fig 59   The front kick is a very basic technique but it is still a high scorer in competitions.*

57

difficult thing for novices to do, especially if they are lacking in confidence and hesitant. The ability to kick on the move makes it a lot easier to adapt to the opponent's movements and successfully score with the technique.

The mechanics of the kick are almost universal in the martial arts. The first point to stress is that the knee comes up high, the leg is kept bent and is then thrust forward powerfully. The supporting leg is also bent initially but it too is straightened at the moment of impact. The ball of the foot is the striking area in competition and the mid-section is generally the target area. In self-defence the instep can be used against the assailant's groin to devastating effect, although this technique is not allowed in contest.

The thrusting front kick requires the kicker to keep his or her weight balanced on the supporting leg, but the push kick version requires a greater lean into the kick. As the opponent is kicked and pushed back the kicking foot simply goes down to the floor, rather than being pulled back. The effect of

this is that the kicker can make a big step forward in pursuit of the retreating opponent.

The front thrust kick is a very powerful and penetrating technique which is fairly easy to use to the body and can be very effective as a means of softening up the opponent. A well-placed front kick to the solar plexus can knock out an opponent as decisively as any kick to the head. The body is the favourite target area for the front kick and one of the big advantages for the beginner is that it is relatively easy to stay on balance when using this technique.

Figs 60–1 illustrate the very powerful rear leg version of the technique where the back foot is brought through and the knee is kept high and thrust into the opponent's mid-section. The toes of the striking foot are pulled back and the ball of the foot is the striking area. This technique is very basic and even the most inept beginners feel comfortable with it as the action (at least at beginner level) is not too far removed from that of kicking a football.

Figs 60–1   *The front kick off the rear leg.*

Fig 61

Figs 62–3 show the front kick off the front leg which inevitably gives beginners more problems than the rear leg version. This can be a surprise technique and is more difficult to anticipate and block since it travels a much shorter distance than the rear leg front kick. To increase the speed and power of the technique, rather than kicking from a stationary posture it is preferable to make a skipping step forwards with the back foot, bringing it in close to the heel of the front foot. Doing this also increases the range of the technique. It is possible to make a jumping step to close the distance if your opponent is out of range. In the left stance take a big step on your right foot and bring your left knee through high as if you intend to kick with that leg, but then instead switch in mid-air and drive home a front kick with your right leg, dropping your left leg into a step as you land.

Figs 62–3   *The front kick off the front leg.*

Fig 63

# The Turning Kick

The turning kick is a natural progression from the front kick and probably evolved as a way of overcoming the opponent's blocking techniques which in turn would have evolved out of defending against the various types of front kick. The turning kick is similar to the *wado-ryu* style round-house kick, but falls in between the front kick and the round-house kick as described in most styles of karate and is very spectacular and popular. Again, the striking areas are the instep or the ball of the foot. Favourite target areas include the neck, the side of the jaw and the ribs.

The amazing flexibility of top taekwondo fighters means this can be a hugely effective knock-out kick when aimed at the head. The balance for the turning kick is a lot more difficult than for the front kick and beginners must expect to take a few tumbles as they try to kick higher and higher. It is on such occasions that one appreciates the value of mats for training! There is though an old adage in taekwondo that asserts, 'Fall down seven times, get up eight' – in other words, never give up.

The turning kick is a basic technique for beginners to study and is excellent for developing awareness of the required action of the hips in kicking. Many styles of karate teach their students to kick with the hips closed but for maximum range and extension as well as increased power it is necessary to learn to open the hips as you kick. To do the turning kick above waist height requires flexible hips, thus to kick at head height clearly requires a lot of flexibility training.

One of the beauties of attacking with the turning kick is that if your opponent attempts to move back out of range he or she is presenting you with the opportunity to carry on the circular momentum of your attack by simply making a step out of the kick and following up with a reverse turning kick with the other leg. Such circular movements are among the most powerful in taekwondo and once initiated are very difficult to stop. The rules stating that the back is not a legitimate target area and that foot-sweeps are not allowed are both designed to encourage such spectacularly impressive kicking techniques. Nevertheless, in order to develop total kicking skill you must also practise stopping the kick and pulling it back as there are occasions, for example, when fighting certain opponents who specialise in counter-kicking, when it would not be wise to carry on spinning into the next technique.

The best way to develop a good turning kick is to get loose and supple and practise getting the leg into the chamber position, that is with the knee lifted up in the air ready for firing the technique. Once you get used to lifting the knee it is a relatively easy matter to deliver the kick. It is important to lean over your supporting leg so as to take the weight off the leg which performs the actual kick, to twist the spine in a clockwise direction to generate rotational force from the hips and to kick with the muscles of the legs.

The turning kick has a variety of applications, but one of the most popular ways of using it is to side-step an incoming opponent and slam the kick into the stomach. The best time to implement this technique is just as your opponent starts to move, contacting with the instep to his or her mid-section and kicking off the back leg for maximum power.

Figs 64–5   The turning kick off the rear leg to the opponent's mid-section.

Fig 65

## Rear Leg Turning Kick (Figs 64–7)

The turning kick can be performed as a direct attack off the rear leg, but then has to travel quite a long way, giving the opponent time to react and defend. One way of speeding up the technique is to make a step with the front leg, causing the opponent to retreat, and follow up with the kick, turning the hips through 180 degrees to connect with the right foot to your opponent's head.

## Front Leg Turning Kick (Figs 68–9)

A third very popular application of the turning kick is executed off the front leg. The front leg turning kick can either be performed as the opponent steps in or, as shown in Figs 68–9, by stepping forwards on the front foot and bringing the back foot up close behind it to reduce the distance. The technique is completed by lifting the knee high, turning and opening the hips and flashing the front foot out to kick to the opponent's head. This technique is sometimes used as an opening shot in competition and when it takes the opponent by surprise it can be a winning gambit.

Figs 66–7  The turning kick off the rear leg to the opponent's head.

Figs 68–9  The turning kick off the front leg to the opponent's head.

Fig 67

Fig 69

## *Jumping, Turning Kick* *(Figs 70–2)*

Still another spectacular variation on the turning kick is the jumping turning kick. This is an advanced technique, and a favourite for breaking demonstrations, being equally usable in competition taekwondo and sparring. It is a kick which beginners need a con-siderable run up to in order to get the necessary height and distance, but which masters such as Frank Massar can execute from a stationary position. As can be seen from the photographic sequence it is a technique which requires considerable athleticism and spring in the legs, but which will frequently take an opponent completely by surprise.

Figs 70–2  *The jumping, turning kick.*

Fig 71

Fig 72

## The Reverse Turning Kick *(Figs 73–8)*

This kick is one which requires great agility and suppleness to execute well. It has been described as like trying to throw an imaginary discus with the foot. The technique requires the kicker to turn through 180 degrees and plant his foot on the target, which is generally his opponent's head. From the free fighting stance it is equally possible to do it with the left or the right leg. The foot you choose to kick with determines whether you spin in a clockwise or anticlockwise direction.

Figs 73–8 show the kick performed with the right leg. To kick with the right foot you would step forward on your left foot and spin in a clockwise direction and vice-versa for the left. The key points of the technique involve lifting the arms up high and throwing the leading elbow in front of the movement to create torsion in the muscles of the trunk and back, and then spinning through on the left leg as the right elbow follows the trajectory already plotted by the left. Throwing the upper body into the spin adds momentum and speeds up the turning action of the hips. It is crucial to get the right knee high as soon as possible, then straighten the leg as the hips spin through. The leg is virtually straight on impact, striking the target with the edge of the foot or heel. Target areas include the ribcage, the side of the neck and the head. It does not rely on the thrusting action of the leg to deliver the power but is rather a scything motion good for coming around and over blocks as opposed to blasting straight through. People hit by this technique often fall face down or to the side rather than being thrust backwards, owing to the direction from which the kick is delivered.

Figs 73–8   *The reverse turning kick, a fine kick in its own right, can combine very effectively with the technique shown in Figs 126–30, the hook kick.*

Fig 74

Fig 75

Fig 76

Fig 77

Fig 78

## The Back Kick *(Figs 79–82)*

The back kick is perhaps the most powerful movement in taekwondo and is particularly suitable for heavyweight exponents who may lack the agility for some of the more gymnastic kicks, but who can generate enough power to compensate for such short-comings. The mechanics of this kick are very straightforward.

From a left fighting stance step forwards and diagonally to the right on your left foot. Turn your back to your opponent by spinning on the ball of your left foot and simultaneously lift your right knee as high as you can. As you spin it is important that your head should come around first to allow you to sight your target over your right shoulder. Smoothly thrust out your right leg adding its power to the speed already generated by the rotation of your hips, aiming for your opponent's mid-section. The striking area can be the heel or outside edge of the foot and

you should always be able to see the kick land. If you cannot do so you are not spinning your head correctly. The head is about one eighth of the total body-weight and throwing the head round quickly can greatly increase the turning speed of this technique.

As a consequence of the powerful rotational force generated by the spin in conjunction with the straightening thrust of the legs, this technique correctly delivered frequently knocks people down or out of the contest area. It is more frequently and easily delivered to the body than the head, which is only a feasible target for the very skilled exponent or when the jumping version is employed. It is important to make a full turn and kick right through the target. Always remember too that when you use this technique you will automatically come out of it in the opposite fighting stance to the one you started in and should be immediately ready to carry on fighting, ready to move into a combination if the technique has not been successful.

Figs 79–82   *The spinning back kick.*

Fig 80

*Fig 81*

*Fig 82*

## Jumping, Spinning Back Kick
*(Figs 83–9)*

The jumping, spinning back kick, although it occurs occasionally in other martial arts, is one of the techniques which characterises taekwondo. Basically, it is a spinning back kick done in mid-air, which allows the person doing the kick to drop his or her whole weight behind the technique. As shown in Fig 84 it is particularly effective when your opponent is coming in on the attack, perhaps when you have kicked and missed, then dropped into a deep stance in order to recover your balance. Your opponent sees his chance and charges in and you leap up and spin to meet his charge with your own technique. All spinning, jumping techniques require great speed as well as split second timing and accuracy. The ability to anticipate movement patterns is also helpful since it can be difficult if the opponent's position changes considerably in the time it takes to jump and spin.

A useful drill for developing the jumping ability to do this technique well is to get a partner to stand in a stationary position and practise taking a run-up into the technique so as to develop momentum. Accuracy only comes with practice and although it may seem an impossible technique to master at first, dedicated training will one day enable you to produce a kick good enough to use in combat.

Fig 84   A fine example of a jumping, spinning back kick that lands just too low, used here to counter a front kick.

Fig 83   A superb example of a jumping, spinning back kick used as a counter to a turning kick.

Figs 85–8   It is often best to practise more advanced techniques such as the jumping, spinning back kick with a stationary partner, so that the kicker can concentrate on developing correct technique.

Fig 86

Fig 87

Fig 88

Fig 89   The influence of taekwondo has spread to sports like Japanese karate,
although techniques such as the jumping, spinning back kick are still a rare sight. The
kicker is Pinda of France.

## The Side Kick *(Figs 90–102)*

The side kick is a useful technique especially suitable for fighters who like to cut down the target area they present by taking up a side-on stance when moving around the competition area. Good exponents can utilise this kick much as a boxer uses a jab to stun and sicken opponents without committing themselves too much and risking being countered. It can be particularly useful when used in conjunction with the spinning back kick.

Facing your opponent left side on, step forwards and diagonally across on your leading (left) leg. Begin to turn your back on your opponent as if you are about to throw a back kick with your right leg. As your opponent reacts to the threat of this technique make a short half-step with your right foot and as it comes down reverse the side kick with your left leg. If your opponent moves out of range, immediately transfer your weight on to your left foot and spin, this

time throwing the spinning back kick with your right leg. These two techniques can be alternated very effectively and are particularly useful for closing the distance between yourself and your opponent. The key to landing effectively is to be able to second guess your opponent's reaction each time, and whichever kick he or she anticipates, switch and do the other.

Many fighters like to stand sideways on to an opponent to minimise the target area which they offer. This posture lends itself to attacks using the side kick, and is particularly suitable for semi-contact fighters who can amass points by gliding or hopping in and poking out the front leg in a side kick action. For full-contact this is not so effective as the amount of power which is generated is relatively limited. Power is best achieved by stepping into the side kick. The side kick off the back leg is more powerful than off the front leg, but as it has further to travel to reach the target it is inevitably slower.

## Rear Leg Side Kick *(Figs 90–2)*

The sequence shows a simple side kick off the rear leg. The attacker is initially in the right free fighting stance and makes the kick by pivoting on his right foot as he turns his hips through 180 degrees in a clockwise direction, bringing his left leg through with the knee high. In a single snap movement he thrusts the leg out straight into his opponent's mid-section.

Figs 90–2   The side kick off the back leg.

Fig 91

Fig 92

## *Front Leg Side Kick* (Figs 93–5)

Here we see the side kick performed off the front leg. The kicker is in the left fighting stance this time, but uses the same leg as before (the left) to kick with. He simply brings his back foot up close behind the front one, lifts his left knee high, the step bringing him into kicking range, then thrusts the leg into his opponent's body, leaning into the kick to add power.

*Figs 93–5   The side kick off the front leg.*

*Fig 94*

*Fig 95*

Another method of doing the side kick off the front leg is to do a cross step behind your kicking leg to close the distance between yourself and your opponent (*see* Figs 96–8). Assuming the opponent is pushed back after being hit by the previous technique he will either continue to try and get out of range or launch a counter-attack. Whichever he does this is an ideal follow-up because if he tries to move back, taking a long cross step will allow you to catch him with the side kick again and, if he decides to come on to you, you simply shorten the step and hit him as he moves on to your technique. This method has greater penetration as well as the advantage of allowing the kicker to really chase an opponent and close down the distance. (This is the same step as is used in the afore-mentioned combination with the back kick and feint.)

*Figs 96–8 Doubling up the front leg side kick to force an opponent backwards by taking a cross step to close the distance.*

*Fig 97*

*Fig 98*

## *Jumping Side Kick* (Figs 99–102)

Another variation on the side kick is the jumping or flying side kick. This is a technique which probably originated as a method devised by unarmed soldiers to unhorse cavalry. Originally, it would have been launched out of a tree or from a hillock, so jumping high would not have been crucial, but covering the intervening distance and actually connecting with the horseman would have been. It is a particularly spectacular technique for breaking and occasionally scores in contest. The problem with it for contest is that it tends to require something of a run-up.

Figs 99–102 demonstrate a version done from a small cross step. In the left fighting stance, step forwards on your right (back) foot, bringing it across and in front of your left foot. Bend your knees well as you step and spring into the air using all the power in your legs. Lift your left knee as high as possible and snap out your left leg so that your knee locks as your foot hits the target.

Figs 99–102   The jumping or flying side kick.

Fig 100

Fig 101

Fig 102

## The Crescent Kick

The crescent kick is aptly named. The kick is effected by swinging the leg out away from the body and then pulling it back across in front of the body in an arc or crescent. If you kick with your right foot you swing your leg out to your right before arching it back in to the target. It is a technique which only occasionally works in contest as it is difficult to generate great speed when attacking at head height, but it is nevertheless worthy of study for self-defence purposes as it can be very useful for blocking and disarming assailants who make knife attacks. It can also be used to build up rotational speed in combinations or to disguise your real intentions from your opponent, effectively allowing you to make a turning step into a reverse turning kick or reverse crescent kick for example. The idea of the kick is to swing the leg up, out and around in front of the body and connect with the inside edge of the foot against the opponent's face as the leg travels in and across. Fighters with very good leg dexterity can use this technique to block kicks and punches, and even to knock down an opponent's guard by striking the arms to leave the head unprotected.

Fig 103  WTF *fighter on the attack with a crescent kick.*

## *Reverse Crescent Kick* (Figs 104–8)

The reverse crescent kick is a subtle kick which can be very useful for getting through an opponent's guard. It can be a very deceptive technique as it is initially indistinguishable from a side kick or turning kick.

In Figs 104–6 the fighter in black does a half-step and hop on his back foot to get in range. Once the knee is raised, the kick is made not by thrusting out but rather by employing a leg action which feels similar to the back fist strike, flicking the foot into the opponent's face inside his guard. Normally the defender is covering his head against foot attacks which come over the leading arm from the outside, such as the turning kick, but the reverse crescent kick can land with the instep, the outside edge of the foot or the outside edge of the heel.

Figs 104–6   The reverse crescent kick off the front leg.

Fig 105

Fig 106

The kick can also be done off the back leg (*see* Figs 107–8) by swinging it through and across as when using the left foot to deliver the reverse crescent kick from the right fighting stance. The kick performed in this way is more powerful than that off the front leg and is equally effective as a chasing technique or a stopping technique.

*Figs 107–8    The reverse crescent kick off the rear leg.*

*Fig 108*

## Spinning, Reverse Crescent Kick (Figs 109–13)

It is difficult to generate great power with the reverse crescent kick, but one way to do so is to spin into the kick. This involves turning through 180 degrees to kick off the front leg or 360 degrees to kick off the back leg. From the right fighting stance, step slightly across to your left with your right foot and spin on the balls of both feet. Turn your back on your opponent momentarily and lift your left knee as high as you can. (If your spinning is slow remember to spring slightly, thereby taking the weight off your supporting leg.) Keep only the ball of your right foot lightly in contact with the ground as your knee comes up. To spin even faster rotate your head and shoulders slightly before turning your hips by twisting at the waist – this build-up of torsion adds snap to the technique. Getting your head round fast has the added benefit of allowing you to adjust to any movements your opponent might have made while you were spinning. As you come out of the spin to face your opponent complete the technique by swinging the outside edge of your foot or heel into your opponent's head.

*Figs 109–12   The spinning, reverse crescent kick.*       *Fig 110*

*Fig 111*       *Fig 112*

Fig 113　A spinning, reverse crescent kick used in contest.

## *Jumping, Spinning, Reverse Crescent Kick* (Figs 114–25)

If any one technique can be said to embody the aesthetic spirit of taekwondo it is the jumping, spinning, reverse crescent kick, possibly the most difficult of all the kicks and certainly one of the most impressive. The action of this kick is very similar to that of the jumping reverse turning kick and they are very easily confused by the beginner. The main differences between the two kicks are the angle of delivery of the kicking leg and the part of the foot that strikes the target. The crescent kick version is a combination of a spin, jump and kick, and if this technique connects it is extremely likely to render the recipient unconscious. The kick lands either with the instep or the outside edge of the foot.

Looking at the photographic sequence, it is very important to study the way in which the various components of the technique combine to generate effective power. The fighter steps forward and swings his right leg and hip through in front of him. Note how the hips are leading the shoulders as he takes the step before the jump in Fig 116. This allows torsion to develop in the muscles of the trunk, and as both knees bend prior to jumping upwards the body is like a spring being coiled. As he takes to the air, the fighter adds the power of the shoulders, driving round to the rotating action. As he is rising he begins to lift the knee of the kicking leg up towards the chest. At this point the foot lashes out towards the target, describing a big arc through the air. At the apex of the kick the foot is still accelerating. As the leg either strikes the target, or passes through where it would have hit in this imaginary instance, it is travelling at maximum speed and the stored kinetic energy of the whole action delivers tremendous impact force. As the fighter lands with cat-like relaxation he is ready to move smoothly into another technique if required.

Figs 114–25   One of the most difficult techniques in taekwondo – the jumping, reverse crescent kick.

Fig 115

Fig 116

Fig 117

Fig 118

Fig 119

Fig 120

Fig 121

Fig 122

Fig 123

Fig 124

Fig 125

# The Hook Kick *(Figs 126–30)*

The hook kick is easily confused with the reverse turning kick as the striking position often looks the same, but the main differences are that the hook kick is more often performed with the front leg and its striking action is generated by the bending or hooking of the leg at the knee as the kick reaches the target, using the base of the heel to deliver the force. It works well in semi-contact taekwondo when combined with the side kick and turning kick. Sometimes if a back kick or side kick does not reach the target because it moves out of range it is possible to put the foot down, cross step to close the distance and do this kick with the same leg.

The hook also combines to devastating effect with the reverse turning kick. Fig 127 shows the crucial point of the technique when, instead of continuing to rotate into a left foot turning kick, the fighter stops the turning action, makes a gliding step with his right foot to get closer to the target and picks up his left knee high, twisting back into the hook kick. This use of torsion, of winding up the power of the body and then unleashing it, is at the heart of the dynamic force which is generated in taekwondo. The combination is particularly effective as it is very difficult for the person under attack to anticipate which technique the attacker will employ. A good way to make it work is to attack with a reverse turning kick and judge your opponent's reaction. If he habitually moves back out of range you can quite often catch him by switching to the hook kick, as the half-step forwards with the right leg will suddenly upset his calculations as to how far he needs to retreat in order to be out of range if you attack with the reverse turning kick. This feint/combination also makes clear the value of being able to kick with both legs.

Figs 126–30 *The hook kick. Compare this with the previous technique, the reverse turning kick, shown in Figs 120–5. Note how the approach for this kick is identical until Fig 127 when the kicker changes the direction of his attack and steps forward into the hook kick instead of spinning into a reverse turning kick.*

Fig 127

Fig 128

Fig 129

*Fig 130*

# The Axe Kick

The axe kick (also called the chop kick) is an extremely powerful and effective kick. Basically, the kicker has to get into range with his or her opponent then swing the leg as high as possible. The sole of the foot or heel is then brought crashing down on the opponent. The head or chest are the natural targets for this technique, but before the collar-bone was made an illegal target this kick broke more than its fair share.

## *Front Leg Axe Kick* (Figs 131–4)

There are two basic versions of the kick. In the first type the kicker attacks with his front leg, using a cross step, stepping in front of his left foot with the right and then swinging his left foot high in the air and dropping it in his opponent's face. For many students this is the easier version of the kick as the cross step gives them considerable spring, enabling them to utilise the principle of storing and unleashing energy.

In Figs 131–4 a slight variation on the norm is shown in order to illustrate a method of creating an opening for the technique. The kicker sets up his opponent by back stepping on his left foot, but as soon as his opponent changes stance by making a step in response, his guard is open, so the kicker reverses direction and steps straight forwards with a cross step to deliver the axe kick.

Figs 131–4   *The axe or chop kick done with the front leg as the opponent steps back by making a cross step.*

Fig 132

Fig 133

Fig 134

89

## Rear Leg Axe Kick (Figs 135–6)

The second type of axe kick is cruder and resembles a crescent kick performed off the rear leg. The attacker, who is in the right stance, steps forward on his right foot and swings his left leg through in a large movement. He then brings his foot crashing down into his opponent's face. The action of the kick is sometimes described as 'dropping the axe', but this is misleading as the kick would lack power if it were simply allowed to drop on the opponent. The muscles of the hamstring and gluteus maximus contract on impact to power the kick home.

## Jumping Axe Kick

Another variation on the axe kick is the jumping axe kick (although it might more accurately be said that the axe is dropped). This type of kick involves jumping so that the kicker is completely airborne as the kick reaches its apex. Jumping increases the force of the technique as the whole body-weight of the kicker can be focused into the heel of the kicking foot as it comes down, adding gravity to the muscular force of the kick.

Figs 135–6   *The axe or chop kick done with the rear leg.*

Fig 136

Once the basic execution of the stances, punches and kicks is mastered, the key to improvement in taekwondo lies in developing effective combinations and counter-attacks. The multitude of techniques are only parts of a greater whole – grasping that whole is the real challenge. To the beginner, tournaments frequently appear to be a bewildering cavalcade of kicks, jumps, leaps and punches, but quite often there is a considered strategy underlying the blur of action. Top class fighters are able to react spontaneously and improvise in rapidly-changing circumstances, but as well as reacting reflexively they must also be able to plan their contests and analyse their opponents' strengths and weaknesses. Competition is far more than a mere display of acrobatic skills and flashy techniques – it is the ultimate test of a fighter's spirit and the effectiveness of the art.

# 7 The Art of Breaking

Breaking inanimate objects such as wood, stone, ice and even glass is a very spectacular method of demonstrating the power and effectiveness of taekwondo techniques. But it is far more than that. Breaking tests the effectiveness of technique as well as the skill and confidence of the trainee and requires a combination of intense concentration and considerable courage. Breaking originated as an alternative method of testing the full power of kicks, punches, elbow strikes and head-butts for use as devastating weapons against another human being.

Although breaking is generally associated with Japanese karate it is principally a Korean phenomenon. The only Japanese style of karate to really give very much attention to breaking is *kyokushinkai*, a very hard style founded by a Korean, Choi Yung Li, who is perhaps better known as Masatatsu Oyama. A favourite demonstration of kyokushinkai's power involves breaking a baseball bat using the shin as the striking area, a feat which communicates the power of the style to the general public fairly effectively.

The three essential elements in any successful break are skill, concentration and choice of material. Considering the last of these first, the range of things which can be broken for the purposes of taekwondo destruction testing is quite extensive: wood, glass, stone and ice in the form of boards, bottles, bricks and blocks are all favourite materials. Equally diverse are the methods and techniques which can be used to break them.

Since the underlying philosophy of breaking is that of testing the power of a martial art without damaging anyone, it seems wise

to consider the safety aspects of breaking. The person most likely to be injured in any breaking demonstration is usually the one doing the break, but the audience also risks injury in some instances. There are various categories of break, some of which are achievable by anyone while others border on the realms of the unbelievable, almost magical. Air-breaking requires a particularly high level of skill since it involves breaking an object, usually a board, which is either suspended by a cord or actually free-falling in space, but while immensely difficult it is not too dangerous. Power-breaks, where stacks of ice, bricks and sometimes even glass are shattered by a single blow, are also extremely difficult, requiring long and arduous conditioning training and practice prior to any attempt at the real thing. Those attempting to emulate some of the more spectacular power-breaks are likely to injure themselves if they have not done the necessary preparatory training.

For the beginner, boards are generally the first things to be broken. The basic breaking of boards usually involves two partners holding a board for a third who strikes it with a given technique in order to break it. This can be made more difficult by adding boards to build a stack. Beginners should never attempt to break anything without skilled supervision as breaking is potentially hazardous, and breaks using the forehead should not be attempted under any circumstances as medical evidence suggests that brain damage may result.

The main consideration when choosing what to break is that of striking a balance

*Fig 137    Master He Il Cho demonstrates a back kick break through five one-inch boards.*

*Fig 138    The same break done blindfolded.*

Fig 139   Master Frank Massar about to break with an axe kick.

between difficulty and feasibility. Breaking a half-inch pine board with a kick does not really demonstrate anything noteworthy – breaking three one-inch boards with a straight finger strike does. The material chosen has to be hard and strong, yet capable of being broken by a high impact strike. Suitable materials are those which have little tensile strength and which are fairly rigid and do not give or flex. Thickness is not always an indication of strength – plywood is notoriously difficult to break, even thin sheets, because of its flexibility and the effect of interlacing crossed grains. Grain is a very important consideration in breaking wood and the direction of force should always go with the grain and not against it. White pine or chipboard are a suitable choice for destruction tests as they break cleanly but hard-

woods such as teak and mahogany are best avoided by all but the most skilled breakers, as the bones of the hand and feet are more likely to break before these do.

Breaking should ultimately be a test of skill rather than just sheer power. Weight-lifters, boxers or shot-putters are also capable of breaking boards just by applying sheer power and blasting through the target, but if the thickness or quantity of the boards is increased they will rapidly reach a point where they hurt their hands and fail to break the target. The reason for this is that they are not conditioned and do not have proper breaking technique. Breaking should accurately emulate techniques used in actual fighting otherwise it achieves nothing.

Having selected a suitable material the next question is which technique to use to

*Figs 140–1 Master Frank Massar demonstrates an unusual break, without the need for anyone to hold the wood!*

*Fig 141*

95

demonstrate your skill. Highly skilled martial artists can break stacks of boards using a variety of techniques, ranging from the relatively staid elbow and fist strikes to ridge hands (strikes using the bony edge of the hand on the thumb-side) and jumping, spinning kicks.

The whole point of breaking should be to try and improve the quality of striking techniques, and ease of execution is a good way of measuring improvement in skill. The fact that a master can throw a two-inch thick pine board into the air and break it with a spinning reverse turning kick before it hits the ground is some indication of just what can be achieved by hard training and dedication.

The subject of breaking cannot be discussed without some mention of fake breaking by charlatan martial artists. It is a sad fact of life that the martial arts attract a fair number of confidence tricksters, individuals who, having acquired some small skill, establish themselves as masters and stage faked demonstrations of their ability to enhance their credibility with their students and a gullible public. There is no legitimate reason for trying to hoodwink an audience in this way and no reputable taekwondo practitioner would attempt to do anything of the kind.

Another theme crucial to an understanding of how to break successfully is that of conditioning. Conditioning is vital to performing some breaks effectively. For example, an unconditioned person attempting to break a baseball bat with the shin would be risking a broken leg. Similarly the hands need proper preparation as the bones of the hand are actually quite small and, in the unconditioned hand, fragile. Time has to be spent developing the ability to make a compact, strong fist if breaking is intended. The conditioned forefist can be a formidable weapon, especially useful for self-defence purposes, but the conditioning process is quite slow and inevitably painful. Press-ups

Figs 142–4   An air break using a rear turning kick.

Fig 143

Fig 144

on the large knuckles of the index and middle fingers performed on a wooden floor help to make a compact fist and to form hard calluses. Training with a straw pad, such as the *makiwara* of Japanese karate can be beneficial also.

Many people do not feel the desire to condition their hands and you can of course use the feet for breaking instead. The feet need much less conditioning than the hands, being designed more with stress bearing in mind. The ball of the foot and the heel are the two best striking areas. The instep should never be used against hard surfaces as the bones in the upper foot are very small and weak and sure to break if so abused. Anyone who has ever done a turning kick and accidentally kicked the point of a partner's elbow with their instep will know exactly why it is not a suitable part of the body for doing breaking.

Ultimately, breaking is a combination of discipline and skill, and like the rest of taekwondo training the important thing is not to be in too much of a hurry. Start modestly and build up. Trying to chop a brick in half after only six weeks' training is certainly not recommended!

# 8 Patterns

*Poomse* are the forms or patterns of tae-kwondo. They are in effect formalised shadow boxing in which you defend against and counter-attack multiple opponents on all sides. Basic techniques have been organised and arranged into logical, continuous sequences in order that the trainee can develop the capacity to make smooth, uninterrupted transitions from defence to offence without the necessity for a training partner or opponent. Sparring was introduced into the martial arts at the turn of the century – until that point poomse had been the accepted system whereby the martial artist developed his skill. Poomse were devised centuries ago as a method of training in taekwondo so that students could safely perfect their techniques. This was particularly important as an injury or death in the dojang would often lead to an interminable blood feud or vendetta in societies where the dominant concept of justice was the retributive notion of 'An eye for an eye and a tooth for a tooth'.

There is a dichotomy in the attitudes of the traditionalist and the sportsperson in modern taekwondo with regard to the patterns, at least in European and American taekwondo. While almost everyone accepts that they are a useful, valid method of training in the techniques of the art, some see them as much more than that. Particularly in the case of the more advanced patterns, there is a body of thought which stems from the Korean originators of the art which asserts that they possess metaphysical significance, though to many modern Western practitioners this smacks of pseudo-mysticism for its own sake.

Of course, as with any belief, its value is entirely determined by the conviction of its adherents. Whether you regard patterns training as pure theoretical combat which provides aerobic exercise or as dynamic meditation is entirely a question of perspective, and both perspectives are equally valid. The important thing is that each group of individuals whether traditionalist or sport orientated should respect the beliefs and needs of the other. To quote an old martial arts proverb, 'The mountain does not speak ill of the river because it is lowly and the river does not abuse the mountain because it does not move'.

The argument about poomse training is completely irrelevant to the beginner in taekwondo since most trainees either love or hate pattern training from the word go. Many beginners, at least for a time, regard the poomse as a bewildering series of complex movements which have to be learned by rote in order to pass the next grading examination. Their lack of understanding of what they are doing is manifest in the way they inevitably try to race through and get to the end of each pattern as quickly as possible, paying little real attention to the details of each technique. Some of course go more slowly, but this is frequently because they are confused and unsure as to what the next move might be and so go slow in order to follow the sequence they see higher grades performing. Eventually, the value of the poomse as training filters through to trainees and the amount of time devoted to them increases. When players get too old and brittle for fighting in competition, as everyone must one day, the poomse then allows them to keep training and learning.

Mastery of the various patterns takes many years determined and dedicated training, but it is its own reward, as once it is achieved the whole spectrum of taekwondo techniques are there to be called upon when needed, whether for self-defence or to instruct a youngster in the right way to do a technique which is proving difficult. Watching experts doing poomse, it becomes clear that the patterns are more than just a series of physical jerks and each pattern has its own rhythm and cadence which must be learned for it to be successfully interpreted or performed.

**The poomse of modern taekwondo have** been repeatedly refined over the years and there is undeniably some evidence of Japanese karate kata (comprising a set pattern of movements, in which the practitioner defends against imaginary opponents) having had an influence, although most Korean taekwondo fighters would be unlikely to admit this. The modern poomse represent a systematising of blocking and attacking techniques utilising the various parts of the body, and have to be mastered in order to make progress in taekwondo. The rationale underlying training in poomse is that continued repetition of quite complex techniques individually and in combination will lead to the ability to perform those techniques under pressure (such as in a competition or self-defence situation) without having to consciously think about how to do them. Practising the various poomse allows the trainee to develop correct form and improve fitness and balance at the same time.

Ultimately of course what you get out of poomse corresponds to what you put in, and although the aim of such training is to refine the techniques until they become virtual reflexes, this cannot be done without making a 100 per cent effort, which means concentrating. Going through the motions of doing poomse without real involvement in what you are doing will get you nowhere fast – it should never be a mindless aerobics drill. The techniques should be done with full concentration as if you really were defending yourself against multiple attackers and the experience should be internalised by serious reflection on what you did well and not so well immediately afterwards. Many of the patterns of taekwondo are rooted in semi-mystical Taoist philosophy and their deeper meaning is said to be far more important than the mere performance of a gymnastic series of exercises. This is not immediately obvious, either when performing or watching the poomse being performed, even by experts, but it is nevertheless an important facet of the greater discipline which is taekwondo for many people.

The patterns of taekwondo are more numerous than the kata of any karate system, encompassing the metaphysical, the historical and the socio-political and while it is a task far beyond the scope of this book to consider these aspects in any depth, the following is an attempt to describe a representative number of them.

## THE TAEGEUKS

The taegeuks are the modern basic training which must be done in order to achieve competence in taekwondo. They are eight in number and are the foundations on which the modern taekwondo trainee builds the rest of the system. The underlying philosophy of the taegeuks is Taoist, deriving from the Chinese *Book of Changes* (the *I'Ching*) and is an esoteric system which cannot be grasped in a wholly intellectual way. One must immerse oneself within it to really understand it, doing as well as thinking in order to completely grasp its meaning. The word 'taegeuk' communicates an idea of universality and of completeness within itself, which implies that the practice of these patterns embodies all things. According to tradition, the eight taegeuks symbolise the principles of the universe and encapsulate these in the movements of which they are composed. The ideas they express are strikingly similar to those found in Miyamoto Musashi's almost legendary treatise on swordsmanship and strategy, *A Book of Five Rings* (*Go No Shin Ro*). This is not surprising as the spread of Zen Buddhism via China (which is at the core of the Japanese swordsman's work) occurred in Korea as well as Japan.

The first of these taegeuks represents the beginnings of all the rest, the source. The second and third represent the clear relaxed positive mental attitude and the enthusiasm necessary for good training. This enthusiasm is expressed by the character of fire or '*Ri*'. The fourth taegeuk exemplifies the need for bravery and steadfastness, in life as well as the martial arts, and the fifth is based on the notion of the wind or *Seon* which is prone to sudden changes in force and direction, like a tricky opponent, or indeed the circumstances of one's life. Consequently this pattern has a distinctive rhythm, switching from soft, almost gentle movements to hard, violent ones. The sixth taegeuk expresses the formlessness of water or *Gam* which is never rigid or still and which remains untroubled, reflecting things like a clear mirror, as the mind should in combat. The seventh taegeuk revolves around the principle of immovability, the mountain or *Gan*, and illustrates the need for static as well as mobile attack and defence. The final member of the group, the eighth taegeuk, returns, cyclicly, to the beginnings of things taking as its motif the earth or *Gon*, the source of all things.

Prior to the emergence of the taegeuks as the core curriculum for taekwondo, students' study of the palgwe group of patterns was the basis for advancement in the art. These eight patterns have a lot in common with the taegeuks which have superseded them, deriving from the *pa-kua* (a series of eight trigrams of the *I'Ching*).

As well as these two major groups of patterns there are various other more advanced individual patterns which can be said to belong to the group of patterns which have a metaphysical foundation. *Chon-ji* is a pattern consisting of nineteen movements which deals with the birth of mankind and the mythical roles of heaven and earth. It divides into two groups of movements which represent the sky (heaven) and the earth. *Hansoo* comprises twenty-seven movements in six directions and is inspired by the nature of flowing water which, though soft, can overwhelm much harder and apparently stronger things. *Jitae* consists of twenty-eight movements and represents the principle of rootedness in the earth, the origin of all life and the source to which everything returns.

Moving away from the metaphysical, *Ilyo* is a pattern which has a spiritual orientation containing twenty-four movements. The title of the pattern refers to the development of a state of spiritual enlightenment which is one of the ultimate aims of the disciple of taekwondo. The student who has attained *Ilyo* is capable of completely spontaneous reaction without any interference from the conscious mind. That student no longer needs to think about how to do his or her techniques, they are as natural as walking or breathing. *Keumgang* is a pattern comprising twenty-seven movements which like *Ilyo* describes the concept of a state of mind. *Keumgang* is the diamond mind, a mind possessing the solidity, clarity and beauty of the diamond, the hardest of all substances and perfect in its geometric purity.

Other patterns are less esoteric and tend to be dedicated to great national heroes or inspired by historical events. Among the most important of these are *Hwa-rang* which has twenty-nine movements and is named after the élite warrior caste of the Silla dynasty, who were instrumental in the unification of Korea, and *Koryo* which has thirty and which refers to the amalgamation of the three kingdoms of old Korea into the dynasty of the same name.

Frequently the pattern is a commemorative celebration of some important episode in the history of Korea, but it may also honour individuals. *Won Hyo* is a twenty-eight movement form which is named after the seventh-century Buddhist monk who purportedly introduced Zen Buddhism to Korea. Other similarly conceived patterns include a number which honour great Korean patriots such as *Joong-gun*, named after An Joong Gun who achieved his heroic status by assassinating the first Japanese Governor-General of occupied Korea. The pattern may be named after the patriot's pseudonym which makes it more difficult to obtain background information as in the case of *Ko-Dang* which is a pseudonym for the patriot Cho Man Sik.

Having had such a violent history it is hardly surprising that a number of patterns are named after military heroes, particularly generals and the like. This is intrinsically linked to Korean nationalism, a phenomenon which has grown out of centuries of struggle for independence against invading imperialist powers, including China, Japan, and more recently against the communist regime now established in the North.

The fact that many patterns are inaugurated in this way indicates the depth of popularity and importance attributed to taekwondo by the Korean nation. There is even a pattern called *Tong-Il* which has fifty-six movements and is dedicated to the desire for a united Korea. To the Koreans, taekwondo will always be much more than a mere sport. It is part of their cultural heritage in a way which is unparalleled in Western culture. There are few phenomena observable in the West which are analogous to the poomse of taekwondo. The only comparisons which spring to mind are the children's game 'ring a ring a roses' which in a macabre way commemorates the era of the Black Death when millions died, and Guy Fawkes' night which continues to celebrate the survival of a democratic monarchy.

Taekwondo's patterns serve a dual purpose in that they help prepare the people of the country to be strong in the face of future aggression, a possibility which can never be wholly discounted in that part of Asia. The poomse are practised everyday by millions in Korea. Every child at school is compelled to practise taekwondo, just as physical education is compulsory in Great Britain, which at the risk of sounding cynical goes some way towards explaining the phenomenal success of the Koreans at the Seoul Olympics.

# 9 Contest Taekwondo

Taekwondo is much more than just a combat sport. It is both a philosophy of discipline and a martial art which entails a system of athletic training as strenuous as any undertaken anywhere. A fit, functional body is built by regular practice training, but even more importantly, in any good dojang the instructor will develop a positive mental attitude in his students and communicate the importance of etiquette to ensure that they are well-adjusted, well-balanced individuals who can contribute something useful to society.

Although some young exponents of taekwondo focus on combat to the point of obsession, the sport comprises much more than just fighting. Competition provides a stimulus for intensifying one's efforts in training and short-term goals on the long path to mastery of what is one of the most demanding of the martial arts. For this reason a variety of categories of competition have been created which have increased the appeal of taekwondo as a multifaceted activity for a wider range of people who can appreciate and enjoy not being limited to straightforward individual combat. As well as actual combat there are poomse competitions, in which the contestants are awarded points according to how well they perform the relevant patterns, and there are also breaking competitions.

Breaking, or destruction as it is sometimes known, is often sub-divided, just as gymnastics is, into different disciplines. Various hand and foot techniques are employed and the winner is adjudged to be the one who destroys the greatest number of breaker boards with a given technique. There are also high jump and long jump kicking events. The high kick event usually involves breaking a single inch-thick board with a jumping front kick. The height of the board is continually raised until a winner is declared. Similarly with the long jump kick, the competitors attempt to break a board with a flying side kick, continually increasing the distance from the take-off point to the target. Quite often there will be an obstacle which has to be cleared as well, which requires tremendous athleticism on the part of all those taking part. The emphasis on jumping is an important part of the art and helps develop powerful legs with lots of spring, vital to good taekwondo.

One consequence of the variety of competition offered within taekwondo is that, since it has a wider appeal than many martial arts, it tends to attract a broad spectrum of personalities. As a result, joining a taekwondo club can dramatically transform a person's social life! However, the area of taekwondo which still seems to attract the most interest and which is undoubtedly the most dramatic and demanding is actual combat.

## PREPARATION

The taekwondo fighter needs to be in tiptop physical condition on the day of the tournament and methods of preparation have grown increasingly scientific over the years. In the early days of the martial arts, trainees tended to believe the superman hyperbole that went with the marketing of the activities, but the fact is that competition is an athletic event and no one can be on peak form all the time.

Of course even at 80 per cent of peak condition many experts would be formidable opponents, but one of the most difficult skills martial artists have to learn is that of peaking for a particular event. This involves knowing how to arrange training-loads in cycles, when to train at a maintenance level and when to intensify work-loads so that you perform at your best on a given day. Perhaps one of the most common mistakes many taekwondo fighters make is that of overtraining close to the big day – in professional boxing the danger is known as 'leaving it all in the gym'. The positive mental attitude inculcated in taekwondo exponents can be counter-productive when it causes people to train hard right up to the day of the event in the mistaken belief that this will see them better prepared to perform at their best. Of course a competition of minor importance can be used as a training event for a later, more important, competition in which case it should not disrupt regular hard training too much.

To be on top form the right combination of training and rest is crucial. The week before a major event should see participants in light training only, just to keep sharp and avoid getting lethargic or even over-anxious.

*Fig 145   Mark Weir winner of the under-81kg class in the 1988 World Open Taekwondo Championships held at the Granby Halls in Leicester in a duel of spinning back kicks beats his opponent to the kick.*

*Fig 146    The power of the spinning back kick is clearly illustrated by this shot of Tony Sewell lifting his German opponent off his feet on the way to the gold medal in the team event at the World Open Taekwondo Championships.*

Many serious competitors hate to miss training even for a day, so addicted are they to its benefits, but the key to a good performance is to ensure that a fighter is rested and relaxed before the event. The day of the event the fighter should be feeling fresh, with his or her batteries charged up and ready for action. If a fighter feels stiff and tired at the beginning of the competition it is unlikely he or she will be amongst the medals at the end of the day. The big danger in full-contact taekwondo is that overtraining will leave the athlete prone to injury which can be a frustrating and discouraging experience.

## WEIGHT CATEGORIES

Full-contact taekwondo competitions (WTF) are always held in weight categories which is a vital requirement as the heavier man or woman, other things being equal, will always have the advantage.

Weight Categories at the 1988 Seoul Olympic games

Males

| | |
|---|---|
| Finweight | under 7.75st (50kg) |
| Flyweight | over 7.75st (50kg) but under 8.5st (54kg) |
| Bantamweight | over 8.5st (54kg) but under 9st (58kg) |
| Featherweight | over 9st (58kg) but under 10st (64kg) |
| Lightweight | over 10st (64kg) but under 11st (70kg) |
| Welterweight | over 11st (70kg) but under 12st (76kg) |
| Middleweight | over 12st (76kg) but under 13st (83kg) |
| Heavyweight | over 13st (83kg) |

Female

| | |
|---|---|
| Finweight | under 7st (43kg) |
| Flyweight | over 7st (43kg) but under 7.5st (47kg) |
| Bantamweight | over 7.5st (47kg) but under 8st (51kg) |
| Featherweight | over 8st (51kg) but under 8.75st (56kg) |
| Lightweight | over 8.75st (56kg) but under 9.5st (60kg) |
| Welterweight | over 9.5st (60kg) but under 10.25st (65kg) |
| Middleweight | over 10.25st (65kg) but under 11st (70kg) |
| Heavyweight | over 11st (70kg) |

That the Koreans still dominate the sport of taekwondo was made very obvious by the fact that they won gold medals in seven out of eight weight categories in the men's event. The Korean women took two golds out of a possible eight, with the United States taking three, Taipei and Denmark one each. The only male gold medal not taken by a Korean went to Jimmy Kim of the United States in the over-83kg class. Such domination, while enjoyable for Korea, is not really helpful to the taekwondo movement on a world scale.

One probable explanation for Korea's supremacy in the sport, apart from being its originator, is the fact that there are over one and a half million adults practising taekwondo in Korea out of a world total estimated at about two million. However, the situation mirrors the state of affairs which once existed in the Japanese sport of judo, but such has been the development in the technical standard of the rest of the world, the European countries in particular, that in Seoul the Japanese only took one gold medal at judo out of a possible seven. If taekwondo achieves full Olympic status, popularisation on a large scale is likely to follow in the West and it will only be a matter of time before it follows the example set in judo.

## STRATEGY AND TACTICS

Strategy is a notion intrinsic to the trainee's development in taekwondo and has to be considered on two levels: strategy within a single contest and strategy in the wider context of training and life.

In Chapter 6 it was explained how certain techniques such as the hook kick and the reverse turning kick, or the side kick and the back kick, can be used together to good effect and at certain times are virtually interchangeable. Having effectively mastered the mech-

Fig 147   *The shin is sometimes used as a striking area but tends to spread the impact force too much when delivered to the body, as in this example where the kicker goes in with a turning kick.*

anical application of such combination techniques a whole range of opportunities and possibilities are opened up for the fighter.

Inevitably, most people specialise in a single technique. It is a curious phenomenon, but the majority of individuals involved in taekwondo or indeed any other martial art will admit to having a favourite technique. Some people like doing turning kicks, others find the back kick to be a particularly satisfying technique and so on. People tend to favour the techniques they feel they can do well. They like to do what they are good at because doing it makes them feel good. Taking a longer term view though, favourite

techniques tend to be transient phenomena. Students can frequently be heard to complain that the technique which worked so well last year never seems to come off now as if it were a factor beyond their control. In a sense it is, however it is to everyone's advantage that this should be so.

One of the reasons that techniques 'stop working' is that they become known to one's opponents and training partners. Nowhere is this more obvious than in the local club, where people speak of techniques as if they were possessions. 'He's got a fantastic turning kick', or 'His back kick is really fast' and similar statements are made every night in dojangs up and down the country. What happens is that the members of a dojang become aware of each other's styles and strategies. In the process they learn to negate them and frequently do this on an almost unconscious level. Consequently, the frustrated fighter begins to feel disillusioned and even despondent. The important thing when this starts to happen is to adapt. Change your technique, add something new, return to something you used to do but have not really specialised in for a while. Taekwondo is like a huge jigsaw puzzle and although it takes a long time to complete the whole picture, juggling with the pieces is one way to make progress.

To get to the very top in taekwondo takes many years and it is a process that requires dedication on the part of the trainee, part of which involves keeping the mind open to new ideas and constructive suggestions. Everyone goes through phases where nothing seems to be working and the successes of yesteryear seem somehow brighter than those of the present. Priorities in life change with age and eventually those who decide to call it a day, perhaps because of work or family commitments leave the way open for those of a more enduring spirit, who go on to become champions and ultimately masters.

Champions are often aided by coaches more knowledgeable and experienced than they, but perhaps no longer in prime fighting condition through injury or other circumstances, although they usually develop their own special strategies to win. It is an erroneous assumption that because someone cannot beat you in sparring or contest they cannot teach you anything. Speed departs, reflexes slow and stamina fades with age, but knowledge deepens. One of the beauties of a sport like taekwondo is that amid the plethora of techniques there is always scope for a new combination or variation in style. The good coach can speed up the athlete's progress

by pointing him in the right direction.

One piece of advice that is always valid, if not always easy to follow, is 'Know your opponent'. Different fighters react differently to different situations. One of the keys to beating anyone is knowing how they will react to a given technique before you use it. Everyone has their own distinctive style. Some fighters like to charge in and get on with it, others are more subtle and like to take their time feeling their opponent out, probing and testing. Some prefer not to attack or initiate anything, but instead to react automatically to whatever attack is made on them. Some are knock-out specialists capable of ending a contest with a single kick. Some are lurkers who look for the chance to counter imperfect attacks but rarely take risks themselves on the attack. Others are fighting machines who erode their opponents' stamina and batter them into defeat. The champion has to have an answer for them all.

With opponents you have never met before there are a variety of strategies which can be applied to help you get the feel of them. Checking kicks and punches are a good method of judging a fighter's temperament. As an attack approaches, slam in a hard kick or punch and try to push your attacker back. How does he or she react to this treatment? Does the attacker back off, or is he or she only too eager to trade? Is the attacker backing off hurt or trying to draw you on to a counter-attack? These are all factors that need to be considered, and which contribute to building up a profile on the person you are fighting.

Figs 148–54 show an opening gambit for competition, one which is fairly low-risk but which can tell you a lot about the type of person you are fighting. As you close for the first time slam in a hard reverse punch or jab to your opponent's chest with the intention of driving him backwards (he may of course

Figs 148–54  Combination techniques utilising punches and kicks.

Fig 149

Fig 150

Fig 151

109

*Fig 152*

*Fig 153*

Fig 154

come in throwing kicks and punches but your response will be basically the same, perhaps interspersed with a few blocks and evasions). If you can force him to step back, immediately follow up with a turning kick to the mid-section. Going to the body first is safer than attacking with head height kicks straight off and also gives you some idea of your opponent's general body conditioning. Assuming he does not go down, which is always a possibility even if it is a well-focused turning kick, back off and observe whether he comes straight back at you or keeps out of range. As you close for the next exchange, switch to the other side and kick to the head. Changing sides often confuses an opponent in the opening moments as does changing the level of an attack, so you might for example immediately switch to the other side and go to the head with a turning kick.

This sequence is by no means perfect, it is only a suggested way of opening up in contest with a view to gauging how an opponent reacts. In two brief exchanges you have tested out his mid-section condition and his defensive reactions to attacks with both hands and feet on each side of his body and to body and head. You can also get an idea of how he reacts to being hit. Does he get irritated when he is hit and attempt instantaneous, perhaps ill-considered counters? Is he the sort of fighter who gives nothing away and just continues at the same pace? Is he one of those who relishes a battle or is he someone who does not like being hit and wants to keep out of trouble? The possible reactions are too numerous to list, but the important thing is that you get a reaction, whether positive or negative, and use it as a basis for working.

## TRAINING METHODS

### Sparring

One-step, three-step and free sparring are all useful, well-established methods of developing combinations and counters for use in contest. One-step sparring is the simplest as your training partner makes a single attack which you counter with a pre-arranged technique. Your partner normally announces the intention to attack and may even name the technique he or she will use and the target area before trying to knock your head off! This might sound exaggerated, but most taekwondo exponents know that the only way to progress is to make training realistic. There is no point in doing these exercises without immersing yourself in what you are doing. Adopting a casual slapdash approach to such training is fatal and not the way to get results. In fact not training correctly is an open invitation to injury and there is no excuse for following this approach.

Every attack should be treated like a real attempt to injure you and handled accordingly if you want to develop good taekwondo. Put everything into it, both when taking the role of the defender and when you are on the attack. More advanced trainees sometimes do not call out the name of the technique prior to executing it, but of course this is only among themselves and by prior agreement. A beginner is always extended the courtesy of being told exactly what is coming next. In order to tax the defender's reflexes it is best if you attack as fast and as hard as his ability allows. Making weak, slow attacks in order to make training easier is counterproductive in the long run and does nothing for anyone's preparation. If the attacks are habitually weak then the defence will end up that way. Heaven help the ill-prepared when they find themselves in a situation where they have to change into a higher gear and they do not have one.

One, and to an even greater extent, three-step sparring, is a demanding activity. It should not be treated as if it were some sort of poorly choreographed dance. Every attack, every defence should be done with speed and spirit. Done properly this is an excellent method of training which ingrains the techniques in the student's psyche. There are an enormous number of pre-arranged moves in taekwondo which trainees practise to sharpen up their techniques and of course their reflexes. One thing that ought to be taught more is the feeling for the rhythm of attack and defence which is part of the key to actually winning a contest. When a fighter is able to impose a rhythm on a match he or she has a very good chance of winning it. In Korea when a fighter suddenly seems able to score at will with any technique, he is said to have 'occupied a portion of his opponent's soul'. This is something which happens to a certain degree to virtually everyone who trains at some point or other; either they do the occupying, or they find it happening to them.

One way to train for rhythm is to practise alternating attack and defence with a partner. The only problem with this is that you may get into a cycle of alternating attacking and defending when there is no real need to go on the defensive. You get used to giving training partners their turn at bat as it were and then you do it in contest where it is a less than ideal course of action. A more sophisticated way of training for the same thing prior to an important contest or grading is to practise attacking, retreating and attacking again, without letting your partner go on the offensive at all. This is more like the kind of dominance pattern that you want to establish in a contest, where your attack may end because you have driven your opponent out of the area, but immediately on re-starting you take the initiative, rather than let him or her get back into the fight. Of course, such training requires particularly unselfish and co-operative training partners.

Figs 155–61 show a typical sequence that might be devised to obtain this result. Initially get your partner to come in without actually attacking and immediately stop his advance with a turning kick. Then get your partner to back off and follow with another turning kick, this time on the other side. Back off as if intending to move out of range in anticipation of his counter-attack. As he comes back at you, cross step as if about to do a back kick with the right leg, to which he reacts by changing stance with the intention of slipping past your kick, but change the direction of your spin and attack with a reverse turning kick to the head. Follow right through with the turning kick, anticipating his evasion and landing in a right side stance. Finish the rally by spinning 180 degrees clockwise on your right foot back towards your opponent, as if about to do a back kick with your right leg, but as he backs off switch again by taking a half-step with your right foot instead of kicking, and thrust out a left side kick.

This is not suggested as a set piece which might be inflicted upon a hapless opponent, it is simply a way of training and opening the mind to the limitless possibilities as far as combinations are concerned. By training in this way it is possible to enhance your sense of movement and eventually reach a stage where every time you make an attack you are aware of an alternative you might have opted for. This sort of pre-arranged sparring is like shadow-boxing with an obliging opponent.

Free sparring is the next step, and the closest thing there is to actual contest, although it should not be allowed to develop into a contest! Sparring is the place where you should be able to learn from your mistakes. The idea is to become wise before the event, not afterwards. It is possible to learn from your mistakes in contest, but is infinitely preferable not to have to.

It is not that important to try and land full power techniques all the time in training – indeed if you do, you may soon find it difficult to get willing partners to practise with. Train for skill and sharpness when

sparring. Of course, against someone of equal experience and ability there is no harm in stepping up the pace, but you should not be trying to knock training partners out all the time – there is no excuse for it. If you are worried about the power of your techniques, practise them on the heavy bag or the focus pads. Light, controlled sparring is the key to injury-free progress. If you go to training looking for a war, sooner or later you will come back wounded!

Mistakes made in training can be rectified, but the first mistake you make in a tournament may well be your last. In sparring you have nothing to lose but your ego. You can afford to be adventurous, so enjoy it. Analyse what works and what does not, look for your own weaknesses as well as your opponent's. Some people avoid practising with fighters who may be particularly adept at catching them with a certain counter or combination. Rather than avoiding such opponents, you should be hunting them out. You can learn a lot more from being beaten by a stronger, more skilful opponent than by beating up someone weaker than yourself. If you train with stronger people all the time you may never get as strong as they are (although that should be the natural result of such training; when you train with good people it tends to rub off), but there is no doubt that you will be stronger than if you had not trained with them at all, and stronger too than if you had always trained with weaker people.

Some of the techniques demonstrated in this chapter may seem artificial and perhaps staged to novices, or fighters from other combat systems who have never seen taekwondo in action or practised it themselves, but they are far from that. They are all workable techniques which have been effective time and time again in competition. The key to being an effective fighter and making the techniques work is relaxation, spirit, physical toughness and speed. When you

Figs 155–61   Pre-arranged free-style sparring
exercises are a valuable method of training to
develop rhythm.

Fig 156

Fig 157

Fig 158

Fig 159

Fig 160

Fig 161

important consideration also. Techniques always land with more power if your opponent is moving on to rather than away from them. It can be a good idea to back off and let your opponent start a chasing combination attack to get him or her to run on to your counter. Feints and movements designed to mislead the opponent and disguise your true intentions must also be studied as they can be very effective ways of drawing an opponent's block. In actual combat most good fighters tend to smother blows with their forearms and hands or deflect them as they move, rather than making rigid stylised blocks.

## Counter Techniques *(Figs 162–9)*

Quite often in taekwondo the first person to actually succeed with a technique and land right on target will win the contest. In many cases the best advice that a coach can give students is to get in first. But for every attack there is a counter-attack and it is always a good strategy to have some automatic response counters to given dangerous situations.

In Fig 162, the fighter on the left launches a front kick to his opponent's body with his right foot. The counter his opponent chooses to employ is to side-step that kick and make a right turning kick of his own to the head.

In the second counter technique shown in Figs 163–5, the fighter on the right uses a reverse turning kick as a counter to a turning kick. As his opponent attacks with a right-foot turning kick the fighter on the right spins anti-clockwise and delivers a reverse turning kick to his opponent's head. This technique is especially effective as it catches the opponent just as he is coming in to attack and will usually knock him down if correctly delivered and timed.

A particularly stunning and impressive counter is the back kick counter to the axe kick (*see* Figs 166–9). The timing of this

attack it must be with total conviction. In full-contact taekwondo especially, half-hearted efforts are often severely punished.

One of the main considerations has to be an understanding of your opponent's movement patterns and favourite techniques in order to be able to anticipate attacks. One of the most difficult things to learn is that quality which frequently distinguishes the successful fighter from the loser – good timing. Focus pads can help develop this but there is no substitute for sparring to really get sharp. The fastest, most powerful kick in the world will have no effect if it does not connect, so the period of training set aside for timing is one that must not be neglected. Many people can perform gymnastically impressive techniques in the dojang, but to make a technique such as a jumping reverse turning kick work under the pressure of contest takes a lot of confidence as well as timing, skill and athletic prowess. Some fighters seem to have no idea of using combinations to set up their opponent for a major technique, preferring to just throw kick after kick, punch after punch and trust that their opponent will make a mistake in trying to block or cope with one of them.

Strategy within the actual contest is an

Fig 162   *A turning kick to the head counters a turning kick to the body, demonstrated here by Ralph Minnot and Seelan Rangaseeny, who both represented Great Britain at the Seoul Olympics.*

Figs 163–5   *The reverse turning kick used as a counter to a front kick.*

Fig 164

Fig 165

117

Figs 166–9 *The axe kick successfully delivered and a possible counter to it.*

Fig 167

Fig 169

Fig 168

118

counter-technique is split second and requires excellent anticipation on the part of the person doing the counter. The perfect timing is to catch the attacker with the back kick just before his leg reaches the apex of its swing. As the fighter attacks with the axe kick he must swing his leg high. If his opponent wants to counter effectively he should start to turn while the axe kick is still ascending. If he does this then he will place his kick before the axe has begun to drop and gather momentum. If he waits until the axe kicker's leg is vertical before starting his counter he risks being caught by the downswing.

One highly important factor in the fighter's preparation for contest is the role of the coach. Traditionally the martial arts foster strength of character and will and an independent spirit. The idea of a coach who takes care of things for his fighters may seem at odds with this, but actually it is not. Before there were coaches there were masters, and indeed there still are – individuals who have dedicated their lives to the pursuit of taekwondo mastery and who guide and direct their students.

These days, whether you are a sport-taekwondo aficionado or a traditionalist, the value of having access to a knowledgeable, objective source of advice and constructive criticism is incalculable. A good coach can bring out the best in any athlete, and will help with such matters as psychological motivation, proper physical preparation, technical refinements, tactics and training-schedule design.

As well as coaching, taekwondo practitioners of the future will need extra help. The stresses of competition taekwondo can be traumatic, much more so than in normal practice, and an important aspect of taekwondo which will need to be developed in the future is that of medical back-up for competitors. Even the hardest, fittest fighters get injuries and there is a tendency to ignore all but the most serious of these and train through the injury. This can be very harmful and can lead to an injury becoming 'trained in' or chronic, which then becomes impossible to completely recover from. Injuries need treatment, they do not go away by being ignored! Physiotherapy is an extremely useful way of coping with most injuries as is osteopathy, but whichever method of treatment you choose, the sooner the injury is treated, the better.

Maintaining a high level of fitness is a good insurance policy as far as avoiding injury is concerned. Entering any competition when not fit, such as after an illness or while suffering from the effects of injury may show good fighting spirit, but it does not necessarily show good sense. You only get one body in this life, taekwondo helps you to look after it, not abuse it. It is incredible the number of good martial artists who will condemn smoking, overdrinking, overeating and a host of other things because they are bad for the body and yet do nothing about injuries which can plague them for years and seriously affect their health. If you get an injury, get it treated.

## OLYMPIC TAEKWONDO

Olympic taekwondo is WTF-style taekwondo. There is no semi-contact event, no patterns competition and no breaking. It is full-contact taekwondo without any of the frills; a dynamic, modern, combat sport. The WTF received official recognition from the International Olympic Committee (IOC) at the 83rd general session in Moscow and also at the 90th session of the Executive Board.

The President of the IOC, Juan Antonio Samaranch, confirmed in October 1987 that taekwondo was definitely to be a programme sport in the Olympics, although he could not confirm whether or not this would happen in

Fig 170　Correct pad position for practising a turning kick.

Fig 171　Correct pad position for practising a front kick.

1992 in Barcelona or in 1996. Only time will tell, but anyone in Great Britain with Olympic aspirations must, sooner or later, join the official body responsible for the sport – the British Taekwondo Board of Control (BTBC). As taekwondo was only a demonstration sport at the 1988 Seoul Olympics only 16 mens' teams and 8 womens' teams were able to take part, although 115 countries expressed a desire to participate. Britain's first entry into the world of Olympic taekwondo was inauspicious, with not a single medal being won by any of the team, but it is probably true to say that a stronger team might have been sent were it not for the political divisions which exist in British taekwondo.

Training for Olympic taekwondo aims to develop fast, focused techniques which have to be both powerful and accurate. Apart from sparring, which is good for developing spirit as well as rounded fighting skills, there are a number of training methods which are indispensable for any fighter aiming for the top. Generally speaking the heavy bag is good for developing power, but for speed and accuracy nothing beats punching mitts or focus pads as they are also called. These are specially adapted glove-like pads which fit over the hands and which the trainee has to strike with kicks and punches. The person wearing the pads, normally a training partner or coach, calls out the shots and positions the pads according to the type of technique he or she wants the trainee to practise. There are special striking pads for doing certain jump kicking techniques which are extremely useful training aids. One of the benefits of practising

*Figs 172–3   Practising the axe kick with training pads.*   Fig 173

Fig 174   *Children have a natural advantage when taking up taekwondo because of their flexibility.*

jumping kicks, especially when using a pad as a target, is that a pylometric effect is achieved.

Pylometrics are the current vogue in athletic power training. Basically, a pylometric exercise involves jumping. Weight-lifters in the Soviet Union jump off high tables into depth squats then try to bound over obstacles from the depth position, using stored kinetic energy. Pylometrics – a new name for something taekwondo students have been doing for centuries!

A combination of kicking and punching drills with pads is extremely arduous when done for three 3-minute rounds, duplicating the energy demands of an actual competition, although of course in competition the target hits back! An additional benefit of pad training is that as an instructor calls out the shots, he or she can see the fighter's strengths and weaknesses and correct faults in technique, stance, guard and so on. As well as being vital for developing crisp, powerful kicks and punches, pad training builds tremendous fitness, so it is doubly recommended. Always stretch after pad work to avoid tightening up and loss of flexibility.

# 10 Fitness Training for Taekwondo

The word 'fit' is a term much bandied about, but when considering the notion of fitness the first question that must be asked is 'Fit for what?' There are hundreds of different sports and all of them have different requirements; the most important thing to aim for, rather than just a general level of fitness, is specificity of training. A taekwondo practitioner is not going to run in an Olympic marathon nor enter a Mr Universe body-building event, so the training undertaken should not seek to emulate those who are, but ought rather to be appropriate to the demands of the chosen activity. A major problem for novice and experienced fighters alike is getting the right advice on training at the right time, but that comes under the need for a good coach – first we must consider the sport's basic requirements.

When then does a taekwondo practitioner need to develop to improve technique? This will of course be a matter of individual assessment, but the five 'S's formula indicates all the areas where an athlete can improve his performance: speed, strength, suppleness, stamina and skill. Ask any top competitor which is the most important of these elements and you will probably find they reply that it is the balance of all five rather than any one single quality. It is no good having inexhaustible stamina and endurance if you lack the speed or skill to score against your opponent. Likewise it is no good being really fast and skilful if you lack the strength to hurt your opponent or the fitness to keep going to the end of a contest. Many contests between fairly evenly-matched fighters technically speaking are decided by superior fitness. The fighter who can endure is the one who ends up on the winner's rostrum. Of course all of these qualities are interlinked and those fighters good enough to reach the finals invariably have both excellent technique and superb fitness. You need to be fit to skill-train effectively in the first place, since the key to good technique in everything is repetition, and repetition builds stamina.

## SUPPLEMENTARY TRAINING

Advice about conditioning is readily available from most good instructors and any supplementary training programme has to take into account the amount of work being done in the dojang. Even very high grade taekwondo exponents can benefit from additional training done outside the dojang, though one of the problems about being very good at something is that it is difficult to get a satisfactory training stimulus when there is no one else of your standard training with you. The more skilful a fighter is, the more relaxed he or she tends to become and the less work actually needs doing when sparring or fighting. Consequently additional fitness work is a must for high grades and certainly for anyone who has reached 1st Dan and who aspires to go further. Beginners doing taekwondo three evenings a week would run the risk of overtraining if they attempted to supplement their dojang work-outs, but they have to recognise at some point that to compete effectively it is an unavoidable necessity. Other benefits which a good exercise programme can have include avoiding staleness and injury and also aiding recuperation from injury. Once having decided to do supplementary training it is a question of ordering priorities by a process of self-assessment and identifying the areas most in need of improvement.

## Endurance

Endurance is one of the first qualities beginners recognise as being advantageous in the early stages of training when they see the black belts spinning and jumping and throwing head height kicks at one another after training for an hour when they can barely move their feet. Running is the simple way to increase basic endurance, but circuit-training has a more specific value for the taekwondo practitioner.

## Strength

Strength is one of the easiest things to improve through systematic exercise using isometrics, callisthenics or weight-training. The difficult thing is to ensure that flexibility or skill do not suffer as a result of an imprudent strength-training programme. Weight-training is sometimes considered to be a panacea as far as sorting out people's weaknesses goes and indeed good results can be obtained through its sensible and systematic use. However, it is a mistake to think that weight-training is the only way to increase strength. Traditional callisthenics can be extremely effective – look at the power and physique of world heavyweight boxing champion Mike Tyson, who never trains with weights! Exercise physiology is still a very inexact science as a result of the huge variation in somatotype and muscle-fibre

distribution in human beings, so it is important to discover the exercises and training programmes which work for you.

One of the great appeals of weight-training though is that it is possible to measure and feel improvements in strength in a very demonstrable way. As you get stronger your physical work capacity increases. For weight-lifters this means they can lift more weight than before. For a taekwondo practitioner the notion of being able to lift more in a single maximum attempt is of little relevance, but if over a six-week period an athlete can go from doing a circuit which takes twenty minutes with a 40lb (18kg) weight to doing it with a 50lb (23kg) weight he has increased his work-load by twenty per cent and there will be corresponding increases in strength and endurance. The technical term for this type of training, where the amount of work is progressively increased to force the body to adapt to the higher demands being placed upon it, is 'The Overload Principle'. The variables involved in any such programme include the amount of weight handled, the time taken to do it in and the number of repetitions performed.

## Speed

Training for speed is often the area of training which martial artists enjoy most. For many fighters it is only really during the speed training phase that they begin to focus on sharpening their skills. Part of training for speed involves perfecting the timing of blows and kicks – often the deciding factor as to whether or not a technique is effective.

# DIET AND WEIGHT CONTROL

As taekwondo is a weight-category sport, attention to diet and weight-control are very important aspects for consideration for anyone intending to be a successful competitor. A 13st (85kg) fighter who chooses to take part in the heavyweight category rather than lose a couple of pounds or so and fight middleweight is obviously placing himself at an extreme disadvantage as he will be fighting right at the bottom of a weight category when he could be at the top end of the middleweight category. Such a hypothetical fighter is in the worst possible situation as the heavyweight category is open-ended and he would doubtless encounter fighters well over 16st (100kg) who would simply be too powerful and hit much too hard for him to be successful in that category.

The importance of weight categories has long been recognised in other combat sports, particularly in Western boxing where the number of new sub-divisions within weight categories seems to increase every year. Judo initially had three weights when it was introduced into the Olympics, but as the myth of the irrelevance of weight was exploded these three grew to seven. Taekwondo has eight categories and choosing the right category in which to fight is very much a question of personal experimentation. There is a 'swings and roundabouts' effect with changing weight categories and if a fighter goes up or down in weight he or she ought to allow at least a year at the new weight to see if it really does suit him or her better.

There are very few taekwondo exponents who could be called fat, but in the opulent world in which we live some are heavier than they need to be and many have found that shedding half a stone can dramatically improve their performance in the dojang and of course the competition hall. When a fighter diets and sweats to reach his or her ideal weight they should feel faster and sharper than normal although in some cases it may become apparent that a fighter loses too much energy in making the weight and

consequently power and endurance suffer. Fighters who belong in this latter group should seriously consider moving up to the next weight category, rather than weakening themselves for the sake of fighting lighter opponents. If forced to move up to fight heavier opponents it is a good idea to put on as much muscle mass as possible rather than being outweighed by just about everyone in the category.

## Exercise

If being overweight is a problem for a fighter, the best way to lose fat in conjunction with taekwondo training is to control food intake and to run. Running is generally the most effective and convenient way of cutting down on weight for competition and has the additional benefit of increasing heart and lung fitness as well as endurance and leg strength. Running is a basic cardio-vascular exercise for almost all sportspeople, but its benefits can be varied depending on the emphasis it is given in training. Long, slow runs will increase basic endurance and burn calories but will do very little to increase the speed and power of techniques. *Fartlek* or interval-training can be used to more accurately duplicate the effects of competing in a tournament where you work during three 3-minute rounds with only 1-minute rest periods in between. To increase sheer speed and power, sprinting can be most effective, and for a spot of variety, hurdles can be used to really put the leg muscles under stress.

Sprinting is not recommended for the overweight; it is a better idea for them to do longer, slower runs and burn off the excess weight rather than subject the knees and ankles to the excessive stresses and pounding of high-speed training which can result in injury. For heavy people who find their joints suffer when they try to run as part of an exercise routine, a good alternative to running is to swim. Also, they might try using a bicycle or stationary exercise-cycle if tyres, traffic or the weather prevent them from going out on the road.

Skipping is another excellent exercise for taekwondo exponents as it increases spring as well as co-ordination and fitness and provides yet another alternative to running. Music can make skipping a lot more enjoyable and helps develop rhythm for training. Anything which helps overcome monotony in training is worth considering and to provide variety a combination of the above-mentioned exercises can work wonders.

## Food

When an athlete is training for competition his or her energy output is of necessity very high, consequently losing weight is a simple matter of controlling food intake. A 1,500 calories a day diet is guaranteed to burn up any excess adipose tissue and is a relatively simple way of ensuring weight loss. Always drink plenty of water while losing weight in order to maintain the body's fluid balance and avoid becoming dehydrated. It is important to remember that the composition of the 1,500 calories consumed ought to be nutritious and provide energy for training. Fats should be avoided and meat ought to be grilled or stewed. Small portions of baked fish or chicken make a nice change but chicken skin should be trimmed off as it too is extremely high in calories. Green vegetables and potatoes provide proteins, carbohydrates and roughage but of course should not be fried or have butter on them. Eggs are a very balanced food with valuable amino acid compounds.

## FLEXIBILITY

One of the first areas where a beginner notices that he is deficient compared to the more experienced members of the dojang is flexibility, which is an important component of any modern sport but in a combat sport like taekwondo is absolutely indispensable. Because of its emphasis on high kicking techniques, taekwondo requires considerable suppleness in the legs and hips. The first thing the average person taking up taekwondo notices is the remarkable flexibility and suppleness of those who have been training in taekwondo for any length of time. It can be quite disheartening for the beginner when he or she realises the vast gulf which exists between white belt and black and even between adult and child. It is wrong though to assume that flexibility is a fixed, determined parameter of athletic performance. Anyone can improve their level of suppleness if they undertake a systematic and intelligently structured stretching programme. Of course the younger the trainee is the greater the opportunity for improvement. Some people are genetically limited by their basic body structure which will not allow them to perform certain flexibility exercises, the full splits being the most obvious of those positions, requiring extreme hip flexibility. In the vast majority of cases it would be unrealistic to expect an average middle-aged person taking up taekwondo to be able to acquire the kind of flexibility exhibited by champions who may have begun training even before reaching their teens. Nevertheless even the stiffest of people can benefit from a properly planned routine of stretching. For the beginner the main thing is to start gently and aim to improve gradually. There are a variety of different types of flexibility training employed in taekwondo and each has a lot to offer.

## Static Stretching

Static stretching techniques involve moving

the body into a stretch position and maintaining that position for a period of time. There are two categories of static stretching: active and passive.

Passive stretching involves using bodyweight, gravity or stretching equipment to reach and maintain a stretched position. Dropping into the splits and maintaining the position is an example of this type of stretching.

Active static stretching is when an extended position is maintained purely through the use of muscular tension. This kind of flexibility is often required of dancers and gymnasts whose activities demand that they display it in their movements. A martial artist placing a side kick at head height and holding it there for several seconds would be demonstrating the same kind of active static stretching. This group of stretching exercises requires a lot of muscular control and also helps improve balance.

## Isometric Stretching

Isometric stretching is a very intense and demanding way of increasing flexibility and is similar to static stretching but utilises the strong tension of stretched muscles to achieve reflexive relaxation. When a fully extended stretch position is reached the tension of the stretch is held for thirty seconds or longer which improves the strength of the muscle in this stretched state, an important factor in avoiding injury. Isometric stretching is the fastest method of increasing flexibility but it is also the most demanding physiologically and should be undertaken in much the same way as any severe strength training routine. This means that because of the long extended tensions placed on the muscles sufficient recovery time has to be allowed between sessions, just as when training with heavy weights.

## Dynamic Stretching

Dynamic stretching involves reaching fully extended positions but using a fast movement to do so. Dynamic stretching is something of a misnomer because in fact it demonstrates flexibility rather than improves it. Ballistic movements have in fact been shown to cause a reactive contraction of the muscle fibres. For example, bouncing into a stretch position was common practice among martial artists for a long time and caused many muscle tears and pulls but modern day sports science has done a lot to clarify the position and eradicate some of the myths. Dynamic stretching should always be preceded by an effective warm-up. In sports such as taekwondo though it is necessary to be able to kick into a fully extended position at speed. Executing a dynamic stretching movement after warming up with static stretching is wholly acceptable and many taekwondo exponents psychologically need to feel capable of making such movements prior to actual competition. It is a method fighters use to confirm that they are warm, limbered up and ready for combat.

Typical stretching exercises often done in taekwondo training include the hamstring stretch, the hurdler's stretch, the front and box splits (including assistance exercises to facilitate the performance of these movements), the quadriceps stretch into bridge and an assortment of yoga-based exercises for the neck, shoulders, chest and back. Semi-contact taekwondo or sparring generally requires greater flexibility than full-contact since it is quite common for instance to flick out repeated head-height kicks to amass points. Such gambits are not really practical in full-contact taekwondo as the kicker is left too exposed and the emphasis is on fast powerful kicks off the rear leg delivered with serious intentions. Full-contact taekwondo fighters are nevertheless generally very flexible as the head remains a prime target area. Almost every session in the dojang sees the taekwondo class go through a variety of stretching movements prior to training, as part of the warm-up. Almost everyone who has been in the activity for any length of time is supple.

# WEIGHT-TRAINING FOR TAEKWONDO

One of the most popular modern day forms of physical training is weight-training and it can undoubtedly be of considerable value to taekwondo exponents concerned with improving some aspect of their general fitness, be it strength, speed, endurance or a combination of all three.

There are literally millions of people the world over who train with weights, for a variety of reasons. Body-builders will primarily be concerned with developing muscle mass while keeping body fat to a minimum in order to display their physique to their best advantage. The Olympic weightlifters and power-lifters on the other hand are only interested in poundages, in the maximum amount of sheer weight that they can shift at a single attempt in any of the officially recognised lifts that go to make up their respective sports. A third category of weight-trainer is the sportsperson, and whether a track or field athlete, a footballer or a rugby player, the aim is essentially the same: improved sports performance through training to improve physical condition. The fourth type of weight-trainer is the man in the street who uses the weights to keep in shape rather than as a training-aid to play sports better.

The taekwondo fighter will generally belong to the third category of trainer, the primary concern being his or her martial arts performance. The fighter will come to the weight-training room or gym with a view perhaps to getting stronger, faster or just generally fitter. However, despite the proliferation of gymnasiums, health clubs and fitness centres there is a definite shortage of knowledgeable coaching and direction on the subject of weight-training for taekwondo.

Of course in the past and even today to a lesser extent, the up and coming taekwondo fighter was frequently discouraged from 'going on the weights' for a variety of reasons. Perhaps the most widespread myths about the dangers of weight-training revolved around the notion that weights will make you tight and give you big muscles that will slow you down. The successes of many superb weight-trained athletes in a number of sports requiring great speed, notably the athletics sprinting events, such as the 100, 200 and 400m have debunked that notion.

The other great objection in the dojang has always been that if you rely too much on strength you will not be able to develop the necessary technique so that although you may have some early successes, later when you fight someone just as strong you will lose through inferior technique. This is a particularly widespread yet spurious notion. Many instructors tell their students to keep off the weights until they get their black belt, the underlying logic being that that way you get the technique first and when you need to get stronger to beat stronger people, that is other black belts, then you can start weight-training if you feel the need. The fact is however, that the stronger and fitter a person is, the easier he or she is to skill-train, and many people taking up a martial art, particularly one as strenuous as taekwondo, lack the necessary basic strength to do certain techniques, jumping kicks being an obvious example.

Many novices in taekwondo are really quite incompetent physically when they begin their training and it is a mark of the value of taekwondo that so many can be transformed by the training. But it has to be said too that this transformation could take place a lot more quickly if weight-training started at an earlier stage in their development. It would get novices fitter and stronger faster, allowing them to skill-train longer and more effectively as their tolerance of fatigue greatly improved. A stronger fighter is a more effective fighter.

As for weight-training making you muscle-bound, that old legend has been pretty well rebuffed on a number of occasions and again it is a question of making sure that your training is correctly balanced so that your suppleness does not deteriorate. Adequate stretching will compensate for any tightening effect that results from heavy weight-training; it is simply a question of remembering what you are training for and not neglecting your stretching techniques.

Standardised body-building programmes are only really suitable for the martial artist if his primary concern is to put on muscular weight and he has a competition-free period of at least six months in which to concentrate exclusively on that, and that includes those aspects of body-building that take place outside the gym such as nutrition and recuperation.

The taekwondo exponent, like the boxer, can benefit from a highly modified form of weight-training. One of the problems the trainee faces going to any gym and asking for a training programme is that the instructors are almost invariably weight-lifters or body-builders. Such people, while often very knowledgeable, even expert in their specialised fields, generally have little understanding of what training in taekwondo entails. A weight-training programme for any taekwondo exponent has to be a balanced programme that takes into account the particular individual's work-load in its entirety, and accommodates and complements his dojang training without replacing it.

The only remaining valid objection to the novice taekwondo fighter weight-training is that, given the rigorous demands of taekwondo training, weight-training on top might result in overtraining. The use of heavy poundages without adequate foundation training can certainly be counter-productive. Heavy squats and power-cleans can cause chronic muscular soreness if you try too much too soon and will undoubtedly cause a deterioration in your actual performance in the dojang. Attempting to practise taekwondo with any intensity in such a tired state is foolish and an open invitation to injury. The rational way to proceed is to start with moderate poundages and build up gradually.

Of course it is impossible to generalise and prescribe a programme which can satisfy the requirements of everyone who does taekwondo as different individuals will demand quite different tailoring. Compare for example the case of a lightweight who is a few pounds away from being at the top of his weight category and who will need a training strategy to improve strength and put on weight, to that of a middleweight who may be half a stone overweight and wanting to come down to the top of his weight category without losing too much strength by severe dieting. Weight-training can help both of them if sensibly planned and carried out, but each will need a quite distinct approach to achieve his own personal goals.

## Goal Setting

Thus the first thing any martial artist needs to do prior to embarking on a weight-training course is to define his or her goals. Why are they going to weight-train? Do they want to get faster, stronger, heavier, lighter, fitter or some combination of these things?

However, training specificity has to be considered alongside phasing. It is more effective to train for one quality at a time and it is usually best to allocate blocks of time to those things you plan to train for. One popular approach is to spend six weeks concentrating on general endurance, with longish runs followed by circuits, another six weeks on local muscular endurance and strength, then a further six weeks on power-training and finally, in the period close to competition, six weeks training for speed and sharpening of techniques, with weights assuming a minor strength-maintaining role, maybe one or at most two sessions a week. Of course the individual needs to experiment and find out what produces the best results for him or her personally. The important thing is to strike the right balance of effort and training in both the gym and in the dojang.

Naturally, the top-flight international competitor will have hugely different requirements to the middle-aged club Dan grade who aspires, not to Olympic gold, but just to being a bit fitter and able to get through sessions in which he finds himself running out of steam towards the end. Physical training is basically of two types – aerobic and anaerobic, and it is your current level of fitness that will determine at what point you switch from working aerobically to working anaerobically.

## Aerobic Training

Aerobic or steady-state training is characterised by the repetition of low intensity movements over an extended period of time. Numerous studies have indicated that the absolute minimum work-load required to improve the aerobic system is twelve minutes a day three days a week at a pulse rate of seventy per cent of maximum. This is the minimum requirement of course and paradoxically it is the fitter taekwondo fighter who has to work harder to improve his or her fitness.

A good method is to use an activity that gets your pulse up to around eighty per cent of maximum and sustain it for an hour. The problem with this is monotony. Hard cross-country running is perhaps the most satisfying activity but many of us live in cities without access to open fields and hills, and the idea of an hour on an exercise bike is enough to dishearten even the most enthusiastic trainee. Programmes can be devised combining activities like running, on a treadmill if necessary, skipping, cycling and bag work, all of which can be done in any well-equipped gym. Again, the important thing to remember is effective and intelligent cycling of activities beneficial to taekwondo.

The first thing to determine when undertaking any form of fitness programme is how far you can go. To do this you need to work out your maximum heart-rate and working pulse-rate. You do that by ascertaining your resting pulse-rate which is best taken early in the morning before you get out of bed. Incidentally, if at any point in your training you feel you may be suffering from overtraining, taking your pulse in this way will give you an indication of whether or not this is so. A higher than normal resting pulse-rate is a sure sign that you are doing too much, and a couple of days complete rest should be taken to allow it to get back to normal.

To take your pulse, place your fingertips, not your thumb, on the thumb side of your wrist, palm facing upwards. Count the number of beats in one minute, using a watch for the purpose. For rapid monitoring purposes you can count the number of pulse beats in fifteen seconds and multiply by four, but until you have some experience, take a minute. The average pulse-rate is about seventy two, but for trained athletes it is generally the case that the lower the pulse-rate is the higher the index of aerobic fitness. Thus top middle-distance runners, for instance, frequently have pulse-rates in the thirties and forties.

Having determined your resting pulse-rate, you can now go on to work out your estimated maximum heart-rate. The formula for that is quite simple: take your age away from the number 220. For example, if you are 30 your estimated maximum heart-rate will be 190 (220–30). Your working pulse-rate and optimum training range (70 to 80 per cent of your maximum heart-rate) will therefore be between 133 and 162 beats per minute.

Once you have worked this out you will know that to improve basic aerobic fitness you will have to get your heart-rate within this range and keep it there for a minimum of twelve minutes, bearing in mind that increasing the duration of the activity by anything up to an hour will bring increased fitness. Exceeding an hour and a half is of little relevance to the martial artist and is really the domain of the specialist endurance athletes such as marathon runners and cyclists.

No apology is made for reiterating this basic exercise physiology as the general level of ignorance in these areas is at times quite surprising. Aerobic simply means 'with oxygen' and any activity which gets the heart-rate up to your optimum training range and keeps it there is said to be aerobic or steady-state.

## Anaerobic Training

Anaerobic training is quite different and will cause pulse-rates close to the maximum and lead to large build-ups of lactic acid in the muscles accompanied by feelings of total fatigue and an inability to continue doing the activity. Anaerobic training is very demanding and severely taxes the trainee, so it should not be undertaken by anyone who has not reached a decent level of aerobic fitness first as the heart, lungs and muscles need to be in good condition before subjecting them to the

sort of stresses involved otherwise injury may result. A typical anaerobic activity is sprinting, especially the 400m. Repeated, fast 400m sprints are particularly gruelling but very effective for improving the body's anaerobic system and tolerance of lactic acid. Often such a programme requires rest periods up to four times as long as the actual time spent training. An athlete doing a sub-sixty-second 400m may need up to five minutes to recover. Anaerobic means working without direct oxygen supply from breathing, but for maximum efficiency both the body's energy systems need to be trained.

Training with maximum poundages in weight-lifting is highly anaerobic, but its value to taekwondo practitioners is questionable especially given the high risk of injury such training brings with it. Repetition squats with a very heavy weight for instance are totally gruelling. The body simply cannot supply enough oxygen to keep the muscles working, hence the intense feeling of breathlessness accompanying such an activity. Shuttle-runs too produce an anaerobic effect and for the super-fit can be done with weights held in the hands to put the body under real stress. Such high-intensity work should only be done once or at the most twice a week, otherwise injury or at least overtraining will be a likely result.

## Suggested Training Programme

So far we have been considering general details that anyone planning to weight-train ought to consider. Now we must look at a tried and tested programme, that of circuit training which can be adapted to a variety of purposes. This particular circuit is fairly short in duration but intense, and is particularly suitable for anyone who wants to weight-train but finds himself pushed for time. This circuit improves strength and fitness, and specifically develops upper body

*Fig 175    Alternate arm dumb-bell press. Ten for each arm.*

and grip strength without leading to a gain in weight. In various forms it can be used to increase stamina, develop strength and endurance and lose weight, depending on what your priorities are. If you want to use it for all the foregoing the overload principle has to be employed.

The circuit contains eight separate exercises: the alternate arm dumb-bell press, triceps extensions, shoulder raises, single arm bent-over rowing, alternate arm curls, step-ups, dumb-bell flys and leg raises, to be done in that order. These exercises are well-known to any competent gymnasium instructor and after receiving brief instructions on how to perform them safely you are ready to begin. Explain to the instructor exactly what you are training for and he or she will be only too pleased to let you get on with it, as long as you are not doing something potentially dangerous to yourself.

Each exercise is performed in a group, normally called 'a set', of ten repetitions,

except leg raises which are done in sets of thirty. The step-ups entail doing ten repetitions for each leg. These eight exercises are done consecutively without any rests using dumb-bells which are gripped at all times except when doing the leg raises. The exercises are repeated twice, for a total of three sets. The tempo of the circuit is fast but be careful to maintain good form especially on the bent-over rowing and curls where there is a tendency to cheat by swinging the weights and getting the back into it when fatigued.

For improved strength endurance and cardio-vascular fitness the circuit should be preceded by a run of between 1½ and 3 miles (2½ and 5 kilometres). Even if you are trying to lose weight, more than 3 miles (5 kilometres) is not recommended as the circuit itself will rapidly deplete any glycogen reserves in the body and if you overdo the running the circuit will be at best too slow and at worst simply impossible to finish, which is not very good psychologically speak-

Fig 176    *Triceps extensions. Ten repetitions.*

Fig 177    *Lateral raises. Ten repetitions.*

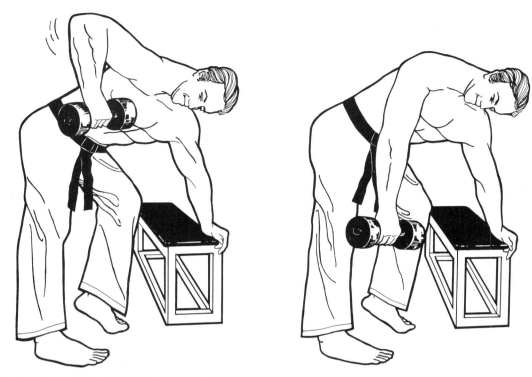

Fig 178   *Single arm bent-over rowing (not alternate arms). Ten left, ten right.*

Fig 179   *Alternate arm curls. Ten for each arm.*

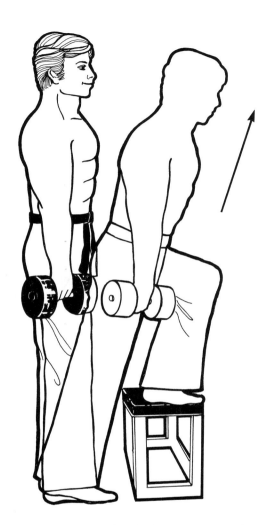

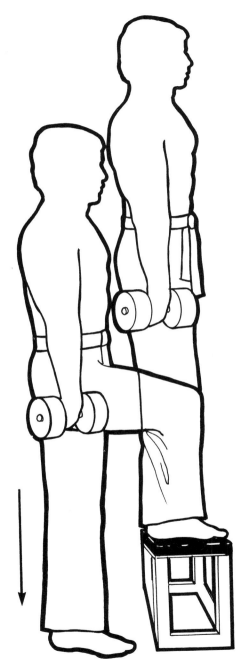

*Figs 180–1   Step-ups on to bench (not alternate legs).
Ten left, ten right.*

*Fig 181*

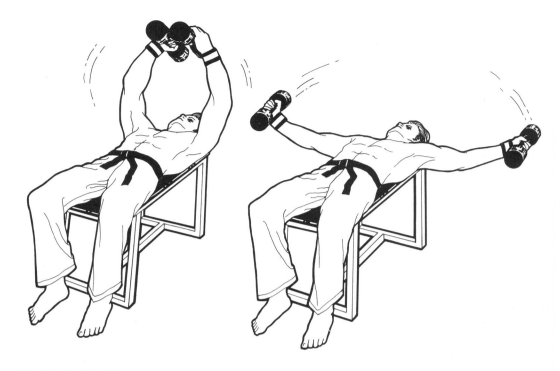

Fig 182   Dumb-bell 'flys'. Ten repetitions.

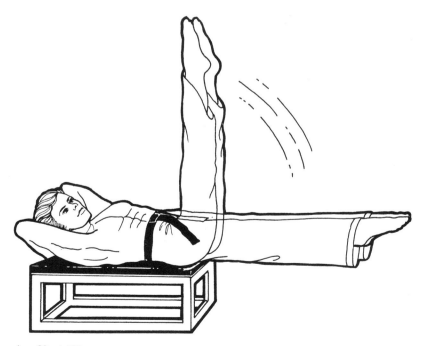

Fig 183   Leg raises. 30 repetitions.

ing. However, even a short rest after the run makes the circuit considerably easier to perform and for an enhanced training effect all forms of taking a rest should be avoided.

Aim to complete the run at six to eight-minute mile pace, remembering the lighter you are the faster you should do it, and that the circuit itself should take ten to twelve minutes. Select a weight equal to about one third body-weight initially. If you can do it in under ten minutes increase the weight by 5lb (2.2kg) until you reach a weight that takes you at least that long to do it. Conversely if it takes you longer than twelve minutes the weight is probably too heavy so reduce the weight by 5lb (2.2kg) until you can get it under twelve minutes. When you get the time for the circuit down to ten minutes increase the weight by 5lb (2.2kg) or 2.5lb (1kg) per dumb-bell.

Increases of 5lb (2.2kg) make a considerable difference to the difficulty of this circuit and bigger jumps will result in a loss of form or possible failure to complete it. To accelerate weight loss and improve cardio-vascular fitness a jog after the circuit is suggested. Ideally this jog should be done immediately after the circuit itself just as the circuit should immediately follow a run, as mentioned earlier.

The post-circuit jog is initially very hard and breathing is very difficult to control, but if you persevere, you will find you actually recover quicker by doing the jog and getting rid of the lactic acid built up whilst running. After five or six weeks of doing this training trainees often find themselves able to run rather than jog and literally raring to go as a result of their increased fitness. One of the great pluses of this particular form of training is that it does not cause the chronic stiffness that often seems to indicate that weights are incompatible with taekwondo.

To succeed with this circuit-training you must have a positive mental attitude and attack the circuit. The equipment required is very basic – all you need is a set of dumb-bells, a bench and a lot of determination. Experiment with the circuit, use it as you see fit. Try doing it three, five and even seven days a week if you are using very light weights. Give it at least a month and preferably six weeks but no longer than that – after that time switch to a different system, you can always return to it at a later date. Some trainees complain of sore lower backs from doing this circuit, usually as a result of failing to observe strict form. If you experience lower back pain do some back raises (sometimes referred to as hyperextensions) but only come up to 180 degrees. Start with three sets of ten repetitions and build up to three sets of twenty and that should take care of it. Ideally you should try to do this in the morning or early afternoon as this gives you a certain amount of recovery before evening taekwondo training. Always stretch after the training and be sure to warm up thoroughly for the evening training.

If exceptionally tired in the dojang, concentrate on timing as technique will tend to deteriorate through fatigue, but always keep in mind that this is only temporary, and that when your fitness reaches highly improved levels you will be vastly more effective. If your sparring in particular is suffering, after three or four weeks try dropping the weight to the original weight you began training with and you will probably be shocked at how relatively easy it seems, which should convince you of your improvement in strength and endurance.

Six weeks prior to an important competition, such as a national championship or a Dan grading, cut back on the frequency with which you do the circuit, perhaps doing it once or twice a week just to keep your strength levels up and there should be a clear improvement in the strength and power of your techniques.

# 11 Applying Taekwondo to Self-defence Situations

Self-defence is a vexed topic within the martial arts. Those who practise contact combat sports are well aware that an individual either can or cannot fight. If someone is trained to fight effectively, be it in taekwondo, judo, karate or boxing, then they can defend themselves effectively, at least up to a point. If, however, they cannot fight, then their ability to defend themselves by performing an ABC of martial arts based moves is highly questionable. Effective self-defence has to be based on either superior fighting ability or on an effective pre-emptive application of intelligence and psychology. Even the best tournament fighters need to appreciate the latter especially if confronted by multiple or armed assailants. It is important to separate fact and fantasy in this area and to ensure that trainees appreciate what is possible and what is not – for their own safety.

Self-defence is a distinct area of study in its own right and many of the techniques of sport taekwondo and the aesthetically pleasing kicks that earn the activity its title as a martial art, are pretty well inapplicable to self-defence situations. A fifty year old man taking up taekwondo for the purpose of self-defence, may never be able to do a head height jumping, spinning, reverse crescent kick, but the point is that he does not need to be able to. Taekwondo is an eclectic system and self-defence techniques can only be taught according to the individual trainee's ability to perform them. When studying self-defence techniques it is always best to keep things simple.

The first point to make about self-defence for taekwondo exponents is that violence should always be a last resort. If at all possible you should attempt to resolve difficult situations reasonably without resorting to physical violence. A second point which needs to be made is that men and women represent two very different categories in terms of needs and requirements. The major difference is that while all men are likely to suffer from male violence at some point in their lives they are, generally speaking, on even terms with their assailants, whereas women are usually physically weaker and are continually threatened by the possibility of violent sexual assault. The average man assumes that he has to do something to provoke an assailant's interest in the majority of cases, unless he is violently robbed or mugged. Women, on the other hand, know that they are potential victims of sex crimes simply by virtue of their gender. 'Every man is a potential rapist' is a familiar slogan of the feminist movement, but of course men too get raped. Male rape occurs especially in closed societies such as prisons and borstals and the incidence of male rape is probably much higher than is generally realised as a result of victims' unwillingness to report the crime. However, in normal circumstances, women are much more likely to be the victims of sexual assault.

Most well-trained martial artists tend to be courteous and polite and behave in a non-provocative manner as a result of the discipline acquired through training. Paradoxically, trained fighters tend not to worry too much about the issue of self-defence because they feel it is very unlikely that they will need to defend themselves in the course of their daily lives, but if they have to then they will be able to. In part this is a result of the confidence that their training has inevitably given them. Probably 90 per cent of people in the modern Western world will never be attacked in the course of their daily lives, but unfortunately 10 per cent will be, and the majority of them will be ill-prepared when it does happen. Another reason martial artists are unlikely to become victims is that they will have the confidence to deal with a situation without having to resort to violence and that same confidence will deter many potentially violent individuals without a blow having to be struck. If at all possible violence should be avoided.

The most likely scenarios for self-defence situations tend to be pubs and night-clubs where people drink too much alcohol and behave irrationally and often belligerently as a result. Traffic situations, where irate motorists sometimes act out of character under the pressure of driving, are also frequently the scenes of extraordinary violence and aggression. Another danger area is late-night travelling, especially by public transport such as buses and tubes where it is all too easy to encounter random violence often of a criminal nature.

Given the abilities which the male tae-kwondo exponent's training for the sport develops, his chief preoccupation in a self-defence context should be how to deal with a close range punching attack and also how to handle a grappling attack. Many streetfights or attempted muggings end up as wrestling matches. Of course a large part of the key to effective self-defence is an understanding of strategy and the ability to apply it. A fundamental example of this would be the realisation that if your fighting technique is not particularly effective at close range then you should keep your assailant at a distance.

The grappling type situation is also a common element in women's self-defence training. If a punch to the face is the most likely form of attack a man is likely to have to face, being grabbed is what most women worry about, whether from behind or directly from the front. The grab is the prelude to being thrown or dragged to the floor, where the male attacker's weight and strength count for more, so if at all possible the woman should counter the assault at this stage and not let it go any further. Obviously, avoiding being grabbed in the first place is preferable, but at least once a man grabs a woman he gives her a carte blanche to defend herself in her own mind because she knows she is no longer 'imagining' it.

Of all the martial arts, taekwondo is one of the best for the purposes of self-defence, particularly from the woman's point of view. Any practical analysis of what works for a female threatened by a physically stronger male invariably recognises that the woman's best, perhaps her only, chance is to attack the man's weakest point. This is generally agreed to be the man's testicles. Other vulnerable and sensitive areas are the eyes, nose and throat, but many women are squeamish particularly regarding poking or gouging the eyes. Taekwondo training makes the task of planting a foot in a man's testicles for the purpose of temporarily incapacitating him relatively simple.

Having said that, there are chinks in the armour of most taekwondo exponents as a result of the rule system under which they fight and compete. Any desire for a really effective, balanced self-defence system has to take these 'rule defects' into account. Any taekwondo exponent facing an attacker who may be a vicious, unscrupulous streetfighter is at a distinct disadvantage. It is a dangerous assumption to make that such an assailant will have no weapons of his own worth worrying about. Prohibited acts in taekwondo include punching to the face or head, sweeps, throws, head butts, falling on top of an opponent and of course all the more animalistic acts deemed to be injurious to the opponent such as biting, gouging and scratching. Unfortunately the streetwise assailant may resort to any of these tactics and in many cases will have done so more than once in the past. Even worse, such individuals have no reluctance in arming themselves with whatever comes to hand, such as bottles, bricks, beer glasses and the like. So, while the training done in preparation for the combat sport of taekwondo will serve the person attacked in good stead, it is equally important when considering the question of self-defence to allow for all the possibilities.

The biggest problem for the person trying to evolve an effective system of self-defence is that an attack can take almost any form and as there are as many defensive techniques as there are forms of attack, predicting the form an attack will take 'before the event' is an impossibility. Given that this is so, the problem may be approached from a different angle. Instead of trying to visualise a host of different possible attack situations (although this has its own merits) it is equally worth while trying to develop the ability to sense when an attack is about to be launched. Among the few groups of people who have repeated experience of such situations are the police and night-club 'bouncers', who frequently have to deal with violent drunks in their line of work. Among such men it is common knowledge that a sudden, unannounced punch to the face is one of the most common forms of attack and features in most cases of assault. Unfortunately for the individual who is not switched on to the danger of sudden physical attacks it remains one of the most difficult to anticipate and defend against.

Self-defence for an advanced taekwondo exponent and a beginner are two very different things. Many people argue that head-height kicks are a bad idea in a self-defence situation and instead they advocate the use of low kicks to the groin, body or legs as the most suitable methods of incapacitating an assailant. There is nothing wrong in using these methods, but quite often the kind of people who 'disqualify' head-height kicks as inappropriate to self-defence situations are those who lack sufficient kicking ability to effectively perform such techniques. There is abundant advice in tracts on self-defence or in martial arts magazines of the 'Only kick below the waist, it's less risky' or 'Aim for the kneecap, it is vulnerable and easy to hit' variety, which, while it may have a nice, safe ring to it, is designed primarily for the unskilled kicker. A skilled taekwondo exponent is quite capable of defending him or herself by delivering a kick to an assailant's head, provided he or she has space to move in and is not wearing restrictive clothing. Techniques become practical through practice. All other considerations aside, the person not trained in taekwondo in 99 per cent of situations is likely to be taken completely by surprise by such a defence.

One of the major problems with writing about self-defence is that the situations that can arise vary so enormously in type and degree of severity. While a kick in the testicles may be a perfectly suitable response if a woman is menaced by a would-be rapist, it is not warranted upon every occasion. There is a simple formula which can be followed in most self-defence situations. All you have to do is remember the ART of self-defence.

1   Assess the situation
2   React
3   Take-off!

This third factor is crucial to effective self-defence. Assuming you manage to temporarily incapacitate an assailant, get away from him! Distancing yourself from an assailant is the best form of defence. If you are not there you cannot be attacked!

## SELF-DEFENCE FOR MEN

The punch to the face tends to be the favourite attack technique of the British brand of street thug or bar-room bully. It is a very simple and effective form of attack which can inflict serious facial injuries. A well-placed punch to the jaw will almost certainly render the person being attacked unconscious and prone to further injury, so it is vital that you protect yourself from being hit in this way. The great advantage of the punch is that it is effective in confined spaces, which explains why so many unruly types favour it. Hook type punches and upper-cuts in particular can be used where there is no room to manoeuvre. Ironic as it may seem, semi-contact practitioners are probably better prepared for dealing with this sort of attack than full-contact fighters as the head is an illegal target for a punch in the latter version of the sport. Full-contact fighters concerned to be able to deal better with punching attacks to the head might be recommended to try some boxing or kick-boxing to round off their ability to defend themselves. The classic counter to a punch, especially if attacked by a taller assailant, is to duck, although it is also feasible to block. Perhaps the most effective response is to evade and block, just in case. Punches can be prevented by controlling an attacker's arms at the inside of the elbows. If there is no room to move to counter-attack with a kick, then elbow or knee strikes are the best choice.

The head butt is a brutally effective weapon at close quarters, but is easily countered by lowering the head as the assailant tries to butt you causing him to smash his nose on your forehead, rather than the other way around. Kicking attacks are probably the branch of violence least likely to trouble a trained taekwondo practitioner as it is extremely unlikely that a street thug will be able to kick as fast or as accurately as black belts in the dojang – to a top competition fighter such an attack would probably seem to be in slow motion. Keep in mind though that if anyone does try to kick you in a street situation they will almost certainly go for the groin.

## WOMEN'S SELF-DEFENCE TECHNIQUES

Figs 184–92 detail some common forms of attack which women are prey to and also some simple counters. These examples are all practical and effective if carefully and frequently rehearsed. The most important thing for a woman is not to panic or freeze. She must be able to react quickly to the threat of danger.

Being grabbed around the neck from behind by an unknown assailant who has managed to get into your car and hide in the back is the sort of situation most people only experience in horror films or nightmares, however it does happen. Car parks at night – desolate, deserted places in many of our cities – are a hunting ground for the kind of miscreants that prey on innocent victims. Simple precautions in such places can minimise the dangers. If at all possible do not become isolated. Go to your car with someone. Always keep the car locked and when you go to open it quickly check that there is no one in the back before getting in. Have your keys ready to hand so that you are not fumbling in your bag for them with your back to any potential attacker. Once you get in the car immediately lock it. Such attacks

Figs 184–5   *Defence against grab from the rear.*   Fig 185

Figs 186–9   *Using the inside of the car for self-defence.*   Fig 187

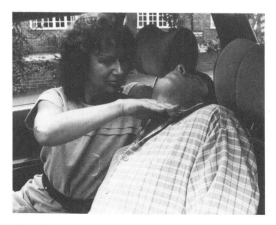

Fig 188   Fig 189

should be considered as life-threatening situations and warrant drastic action. There are cases on record where the double-finger strike to the eyes has successfully been employed in real life and death situations. One woman in America partially blinded an attacker who was later arrested by police and confessed that he would have killed the woman had she not managed to defend herself and escape.

In Figs 184–5 the woman reacts instantly to being grabbed and before her attacker has a chance to tighten his grip she twists in her seat, avoiding the danger of direct pressure on her throat, and immediately jabs her assailant in the eyes with her fingers. This should blind her attacker at least temporarily and give her the chance to get out of the car and run for help. The eyes are extremely sensitive and vulnerable and if done with great force this technique will cause permanent eye damage. It should never be practised with any degree of contact on a partner. A suitable alternative for actually practising striking something with this technique would be a bean bag hung from a cord.

Everyone should be aware of the dangers of picking up hitch-hikers and very few women would be rash enough to stop to pick up a total stranger. A similar danger exists in the case where a woman may give a lift to a man she only vaguely knows. It is a well-publicised statistic that the majority of rape victims know their attackers. A woman is probably more likely to become a victim if she assumes a passive role in such situations, such as when she accepts a lift from a man she does not really know that well, say a friend of a friend met at a party. These situations are often compounded when the man has been drinking.

In Figs 186–9 the woman is pictured in the driver's seat, but the defence she employs when she feels herself to be sexually threatened is equally practicable from the passenger seat. She grabs her attacker's hair, pulling

back his head to expose his throat which she then strikes with a reverse knife-hand, finally banging his head on the dashboard before escaping from the car. As a passenger it is actually easier for the woman, psychologically at least, to get out of the car after the incident. If she is driving she has to decide between either trying to get the man out of her car – no easy task – or abandoning the vehicle and running for help. Of course it would be far better to take the necessary precautions to ensure that the situation does not arise in the first place.

When driving, especially in built up areas, it is always judicious to keep car doors and windows locked as there is the danger that an assailant will simply open the door and get in. Using common sense and taking the necessary precautions in such situations can forestall many attacks, precluding the need to physically defend yourself.

Another form of attack, shown in Figs 190–2, is the rear strangle, in this case with straight arms. This is a relatively easy grip to break. The woman simply stoops and turns 180 degrees in an anticlockwise direction, twisting the attacker's wrists and breaking his grip. From this position she immediately fires an upper-cut into his testicles, which should cause him to let go, allowing her to run away to a place of safety.

## KNIFE ATTACKS

The armed attack is another category of assault which requires an effective response. Both men and women are potential victims of armed attackers and the most likely weapon any of us are likely to find ourselves facing is the knife. The crucial element in defending against knife attacks is, above all else, speed of reaction. The best martial artist in the world can only successfully defend against knife attack by being quicker and more

Figs 190–2  Defence against a rear
strangle attack.

Fig 191

Fig 192

decisive than his or her attacker. In a sense you must never lose sight of the fact that although the knife is a dangerous weapon, it becomes more or less dangerous depending upon who is wielding it. If an attacker is basically an untrained person who happens to have decided to carry a knife because he knows its value in terms of psychological intimidation (for example, as a means of bullying victims into handing over money) you are in a quite different situation than if he is a psychopath who has learned how to use the knife by experience.

Many martial artists practise techniques using knives, normally from the point of view of defending against attackers so armed. Unfortunately the chances of being attacked by someone armed with a knife seem to be growing all the time. The situation is not helped by individuals on the fringe of the martial arts fraternity who go in for 'free fighting' with naked blades, nor by some of the unbelievably irresponsible literature which is so readily available.

Generally, a knife attack, once it goes beyond the threat stage, will take the form of either a slashing attack or a stabbing attack. While the slash is not generally as lethal as the

stab there is always the possibility of death from blood loss, and rapid death at that if a major artery is severed, making it highly dangerous. With slashing attacks the face is often a prime target and if successful, serious disfigurement can result. It is important though that in seeking to protect the face the throat does not become exposed. Many people, particularly karateka who are conditioned to snap the head back to avoid punches, risk offering the throat which is an even more vulnerable and potentially fatal target area to the attacker. Always keep the head down when confronting an assailant armed with a knife and keep the neck covered at all times. The neck/throat area figures surprisingly highly in the statistics for knife woundings, but it is often the case that this is a direct result of attempting to dodge a slash at the face. This also applies when the attacker stabs with a broken bottle or glass.

Another factor worthy of consideration is the danger of fixing the attention on the knife. The untrained person invariably cannot see beyond the threat represented by the blade and frequently makes foolish errors of judgement in trying to wrest the weapon from the person wielding it. The attacker has to be the focus of your attention as much as the knife since although it is unlikely that a man carrying a knife is going to try and punch or kick his intended victim, the possibility cannot be ignored. Normally the knife will be the focus of his attention every bit as much as it is his intended victim's.

However, it is vital that you immediately identify the type of weapon the knife is. The reasons for this are many, but most importantly the type of knife and the way in which it is held can indicate what form an attack might take. The Stanley knife for instance is ineffective as far as being a stabbing weapon goes but can inflict actual damage when used to slash with. A stiletto on the other hand does its deadly work with the point so a stabbing attack is much more probable, whereas something bigger like a machete is essentially a chopping weapon which, while giving the attacker a daunting range advantage, does need to be drawn back in order for power to be generated.

Training for knife attacks is highly specialised and needs to be approached very seriously. Initially you have to make a choice as to whether or not to train with a real or a dummy knife. Training with a dummy knife has the obvious advantage of safety but it can lead to sloppiness and complacency as there is little real sense of danger. Probably it is better for less experienced people to begin with a dummy knife, progressing to working with an equally experienced partner at about first Dan level. Beginners should never be allowed to use a real blade under any circumstances, either in the role of *tori* or *uke*. Using a real knife makes the situation real and any training tends to be done with full concentration, but the dangers are obvious. The competent instructor has a responsibility to ensure that only safe and workable techniques are practised when real knives are being used. Spontaneity and inventiveness as in a free sparring situation ought not to be

encouraged against a live blade as it frequently leads to people cutting themselves. Such training, which can be useful to sharpen the reflexes and give the trainee some idea of the difficulties involved in defending against an attacker armed with a knife, is best done with a dummy blade.

When practising the techniques demonstrated in the photographic sequences in this chapter it is important to pay attention to the study of *omgyo* or distance evaluation. You have to learn to recognise when you and your opponent are within each others' effective striking range. Always be aware of the extended reach afforded by the knife and take into consideration your options in terms of evasive movement. The dojang practice needs to be relevant to a real situation; quite often in a crowded environment such as a bar or nightclub it may be impossible to move either laterally or backwards, and the only option available may be to stand your ground – not an enviable position to be in. Such conditions are among the few sets of circumstances where it might even prove necessary to actually move into the attacker. This is not generally a sound strategy for the reason that if you are moving on to a knife thrust its effectiveness will be enhanced just as being hit with a kick as you are moving on to it doubles the force whereas moving away, you only get caught a glancing blow.

Mugging and demanding money with menaces are not new phenomena – the eighteenth century had its mashers and footpads and highwaymen who frequently stopped people with the chilling demand 'your money or your life'. While this may have a comic ring to it in the modern day, the message, when a street thug pulls out a knife and says, 'hand over your cash', is the same. As has been said before, discretion is often the better part of valour and if a potentially lethal situation can be avoided by handing over ten, twenty, or thirty pounds, or whatever amount you may be carrying, however humiliating such a capitulation may be, then it may be the most pragmatic way to deal with the situation. Ultimately it is a decision the individual has to make when the situation arises. Any student who has not reached at least Dan grade in taekwondo would probably be well advised to hand over some money. Even Dan grades should remember that being a black belt does not make you invulnerable, it will not stop you from bleeding when slashed or stabbed with a knife.

Talking with a potential assailant armed with a knife can often be more productive than automatically attempting to disarm and counter-attack him. An understanding of the psychology of the assailant is important and you need to be able to assess the type of person you find yourself confronted with. Is he nervous and unpredictable, or cool, calm and collected? Has he been taking drugs? Is he desperate or emotionally out of control? These can all be important considerations in planning your strategy for dealing with the situation.

Some muggers, perhaps the more intelligent variety, are actually susceptible to negotiation. For them mugging is essentially a business, it is their way of making a living. Stories have filtered through in the national press of a phenomenon which has been dubbed 'Yuppie tax'. Basically this has involved thugs holding affluent yuppie types at knifepoint, going through their wallets and taking a certain amount out of the wallet, perhaps 90 per cent, then returning it credit cards and all, and walking away. The thinking behind this sort of crime is that it is a mistake to chop down a tree just to get the fruit when it can be picked and picked again and again. It also renders the mugger in a more favourable light – some victims have referred to the event as 'a civilised mugging'. They are actually grateful, even appreciative in some cases to have got away without being hurt, even though they get robbed. Such types are quite happy to hand over the money as it probably amounts to less than they pay in parking fines in the course of a year! This is a philosophy of expediency on the part of the victim though and becomes useless when confronted by a psychopath who enjoys cutting people, or a drunk who cannot be reasoned with, so its value for self-defence is rather limited.

Other muggers can be intimidated into backing off, and the less intelligent knife carrier can often be tricked or bluffed. This requires a lot of confidence on the part of the intended victim. One taekwondo green belt when threatened with a knife calmly informed his would-be assailant that he was a 4th Dan and that if anyone was going to get cut it would not be him and that he was making a citizen's arrest. The mugger turned and ran as fast as his legs could carry him. Quick thinking can often preclude the necessity for physical action, but as with any bluff there is always the danger that it can backfire. In the final analysis there is no substitute for being sufficiently well trained and psychologically prepared to deal decisively with the situation when it becomes physical.

While some would argue that a slash to the face may often be more of a threat rather than an actual attack (some muggers cut the air in order to intimidate their prey into handing over their money), the statistics seem to indicate that the face is a common target. Stabbing attacks to the face or to the body are potentially lethal and should be treated as such. In any such instance if you possibly can, arm yourself, preferably with something that gives you striking range, such as a long piece of wood, a chair, or something which can be thrown, such as a rock or a bottle. This advice is not intended to encourage uncivilised behaviour but there is nothing civilised about a knife attack and sometimes you have to fight fire with fire. However, carrying a knife for self-defence is totally unacceptable while the use of drastic force is morally though not always legally justified.

With all techniques for dealing with knife attacks in practice, control should be a prime concern, but in defending against a street knife attack the taekwondo student should aim to inflict as much pain and damage as possible to disable the attacker in the shortest possible time. Always bear in mind that the law allows the use of reasonable force in self-defence and that when dealing with an attacker armed with a knife you are acting in fear of your life. The normal restraint which typifies taekwondo exponents when dealing with less serious assaults is something they simply cannot afford in what is from the outset a life-threatening situation.

Which technique to use in a knife-attack situation will be determined by factors such as the nature of attacker, the place the attack happens, the clothes you are wearing, the type of knife being used and so on. Leaving these aside for a moment, the main priority should always be to remove the danger from the situation. There are two approaches to the problem. The first considers the knife to be the problem or source of the danger and the strategy adopted then is to take the knife and disarm the attacker. The second approach is to treat the attacker as the danger, not the knife, and the logical thing to do in this instance is to knock him out. The fact that an assailant is carrying a knife makes him much more dangerous, but it does not make him any more able to withstand a full power blow, be it a kick or whatever. The main concern, which is to avoid getting stabbed, remains the same whichever approach is adopted. Only use techniques with which you are completely familiar and in which you have total confidence. Once you decide to defend yourself, incapacitate your attacker as quickly as possible. There are no second chances in such situations.

# Appendix

## Results of the Taekwondo Event at the 1988 Seoul Olympics

### Men

| Category | Position | Name | Country |
|---|---|---|---|
| Finweight | Gold | Tae Ho Kwon | Korea |
| | Silver | Juan Moreno | USA |
| | Bronze | Enrique Torroella | Mexico |
| | | Bidhan Lama | Nepal |
| Flyweight | Gold | Tae Kyung Ha | Korea |
| | Silver | Gabriel Garcia | Spain |
| | Bronze | Adel Darraj | Bahrain |
| | | Ishan Abushekah | Jordan |
| Bantamweight | Gold | Yong Suk Ji | Korea |
| | Silver | Jose Sanabria | Spain |
| | Bronze | Feisal Danesh | Iran |
| | | Jan Won Lee | USA |
| Featherweight | Gold | Myung Sam Chang | Korea |
| | Silver | Cengiz Yagliz | Turkey |
| | Bronze | Samer Kamal | Jordan |
| | | Ibrahim Al Gafar | Kuwait |
| Lightweight | Gold | Bong Kwon Park | Korea |
| | Silver | Jose Maria Sanchez | Spain |
| | Bronze | Manuel Jurado | Mexico |
| | | Greg Baker | USA |
| Welterweight | Gold | Kook Hyun Chung | Korea |
| | Silver | Luigi D'Oriano | Italy |
| | Bronze | Tsung Che Wu | Taipei |
| | | Jay Warwick | USA |
| Middleweight | Gold | Kye Haeng Lee | Korea |
| | Silver | Amir Hussein | Egypt |
| | Bronze | Marcus Woznicki | East Germany |
| | | Metin Sahin | Turkey |

| Category | Position | Name | Country |
|----------|----------|------|---------|
| Heavyweight | Gold | Jimmy Kim | USA |
| | Silver | Jong Suk Kim | Korea |
| | Bronze | Jose Luis Alvarez | Spain |
| | | Michael Arndt | East Germany |

## Women

| Category | Position | Name | Country |
|----------|----------|------|---------|
| Finweight | Gold | Chin Yu Fang | Taipei |
| | Silver | Hwa Jin Lee | Korea |
| | Bronze | Vasugi Marathamuthu | Malaysia |
| | | Monica Torres | Mexico |
| Flyweight | Gold | Nan Yool Choo | Korea |
| | Silver | Maria Angela Naranjo | Spain |
| | Bronze | Yun Yao Pai | Taipei |
| | | Mayumi Pejo | USA |
| Bantamweight | Gold | Yi An Chen | Taipei |
| | Silver | Debra Holloway | USA |
| | Bronze | Josefina Lopez | Spain |
| | | Sun Young Park | Korea |
| Featherweight | Gold | Annemette Christiansen | Denmark |
| | Silver | Zuleyha Tan | Turkey |
| | Bronze | Amparo Dolls | Spain |
| | | So Young Kim | Korea |
| Lightweight | Gold | Dana Hee | USA |
| | Silver | Karin Schwarz | Denmark |
| | Bronze | Jolanda Van Duren | Holland |
| | | Jiun Feng Chen | Taipei |
| Welterweight | Gold | Arlene Limas | USA |
| | Silver | Ji Sook Kim | Korea |
| | Bronze | Coral Bistuer | Spain |
| | | Sonny Seidel | West Germany |
| Middleweight | Gold | Hyun Hee Kim | Korea |
| | Silver | Margaretha De Johng | Holland |
| | Bronze | Elena Navaz | Spain |
| | | Sharon Jewel | USA |
| Heavyweight | Gold | Lynette Love | USA |
| | Silver | Yoon Jung Jang | Korea |
| | Bronze | Yvonne Franssen | Canada |
| | | Ute Guester | East Germany |

# Glossary of Korean Taekwondo Terminology

## Note

Because there is no standardised English phonetic transcription of Korean characters, there is some variety in the terminology used in the disparate schools of taekwondo. The various techniques have been named in English throughout the book to avoid any confusion. The following glossary should be of help to students of taekwondo keen to master the Korean terminology, whichever system they are training within.

**Ageum son** An open-handed technique which utilises the ridge of the index finger and the inside edge of the thumb, usually applied against the throat.

**An chig** An internal line strike directed to the centre of an assailant's body.

**An makagi** The inner block. (Also written **An-makki** or **An marki** The words makki, marki, and makagi can effectively be considered as synonyms throughout the glossary.)

**Annun sogi** The straddle stance, both feet shoulder width or wider apart and pointing forwards with the knees well bent.

**An palja sogi** A variant of the ready stance in which the toes are turned slightly inwards.

**Anuro chagi** Generic term for kicks delivered to the knee or lower leg.

**Anuro markgi** Inward travelling block. (Also written **Anuro marki**.)

**Apcha busigi** Front snap kick where the kicking foot is pulled back immediately.

**Ap chagi** Generic term for front kicks.

**Ap cha olligi** Block using the foot.

**Apchook** The ball of the foot, used as the striking area for many kicks.

**Ap choomuk** The forefist.

**Ape chigi** A direct frontal strike.

**Apkoobi** A lunge punch where the striking hand is the same side as the front foot, e.g. left foot, left hand.

**Ap makgi** A block applied when square-on to an opponent.

**Ap seogi** A short version of the forward stance with about 65 per cent of the bodyweight on the front leg. (Also written **Ap sogi**.)

**Arae** The groin and lower areas of the body.

**Arae makki** Lower, or downward block.

**Aun no gyo** A breathing exercise performed by squatting down low and inhaling then rising up on to the tips of the toes and reaching straight overhead with both hands and exhaling.

**Baekjul boolgool** Fighting attitude characterised by fearlessness, confidence and determination.

**Bakat makgi** A block delivered to the outside edge of an arm or leg.

**Bakkat chigi** An outward travelling strike.

**Bal** The foot.

**Baldadak** The inside edge of the foot.

**Baldeung** The instep. (Also written **Baldung** and **Baltung**.)

**Bal dul gi** Footsweep avoidance.

**Bal gurum** Footwork.

**Balkal**   The outside edge of the foot. (Also written **Balnal** and **Jodko**.)

**Balkut**   The toes.

**Bal twikumchi**   The heel when used as the striking area for a kick.

**Bam joomeok**   Punch using the extended knuckle of the middle finger.

**Bandae chirugi**   The stepping punch.

**Bandae dollyo chagi**   The reverse turning kick used when the target is to the side or rear.

**Bandae dollyo goro chagi**   The reverse hook kick.

**Bandal chagi**   The crescent kick.

**Bandal jireugi**   A round-house punch or hook.

**Bandal son**   A reverse knife-hand strike.

**Bang au**   Defensive measures.

**Bang jayoo daeryon**   Semi-free sparring, where students alternate in attacking and defensive roles.

**Bangkyuk**   Counter technique.

**Baro jireugi**   The reverse punch.

**Batang son**   The heel of the palm strike.

**Beom seogi**   Tiger stance.

**Bituro chagi**   Twisting kick.

**Bokboo**   The centre, the Korean equivalent to the Japanese concept of the *Hara*, with the lower abdomen representing the centre of man's physical being and source of life.

**Bong**   A six foot wooden staff used in some Korean weapons schools.

**Butjaba makgi**   Block and grab technique also known as a grasping block.

**Butjapgo chagi**   Kicking one assailant while holding on to another.

**Cha bapgi**   Stamping kick to the instep.

**Chagi**   All kicking techniques.

**Cha mum chagi**   Use of a kicking technique for the purposes of blocking.

**Chang Kwon**   The palm heel strike.

**Chang mu kwan**   A martial arts academy founded in 1946 by Byun In Yoon which refused to be incorporated into General Choi's taekwondo.

**Charyot seogi**   The attention stance, heels together, feet pointing out at 45 degrees.

**Cheong kwon**   A pattern comprising twenty-seven movements.

**Chigi**   The collective term for striking techniques such as punches and chops.

**Chi jireugi**   Upper-cut strike.

**Chodan**   First black belt grade, or first Dan.

**Chojum**   Focus, the principle of directing maximum energy into a single point for maximum effectiveness.

**Chongul**   A forward stance where the weight is equally distributed over both legs.

**Chon ji**   A pattern named after the creation of humanity.

**Chookya makgi**   Overhead block against downcoming strike such as axe kick.

**Choongdan**   The mid-section of the body, from the base of the neck to the waist.

**Choong sim**   Centre of gravity.

**Chung do kwan**   A martial arts academy founded by Won kook Lee in 1945.

**Chung ga**   To add power to a technique, by using another limb to back it up.

**Chwa**   Left.

**Daebee Guard**   The position of the hands and body for self-protection when fighting.

**Daebee marki**   Block employing both hands in front of the chest.

**Daeryon**   Collective term for all varieties of sparring.

**Dallyon joo**   Punching post used for conditioning the striking surfaces of the hands and feet in order to form calluses.

**Danjun ki**   Breathing exercises to assist the development of *ki* or internal energy.

**Dari**   Leg.

**Dari pyogi**   Leg stretching exercises.

**Ddee**   The belt.

**Dduiyo chagi**   Jumping kicks.

**Dee jeea jireugi**   Short-range punching techniques for inside fighting.

**Deemyun bandae dollyo chagi**   The flying reverse turning kick. (The word Twimyun is synonymous with Deemyun and can be considered interchangeable for all the following techniques.)

**Deemyun bituro chagi** Flying twisting kick performed to the front.

**Deemyun chagi** A collective term for all flying kicks.

**Deemyun dollyo chagi** Flying turning kick.

**Deemyun yopcha jireugi** The flying side kick.

**Deung joomeok** The back fist.

**Dobok** A white cotton jacket and trousers tied with a belt, worn by taekwondo students as a training uniform.

**Dojang** The training hall or gymnasium.

**Dolgi** Turning.

**Dolli myo makgi** Circular block.

**Dollyo chagi** Turning kick. (Also written **Tollyo chagi**.)

**Dollyo jireugi** Turning punch or round-house hook.

**Doobaldangsang** Flying kick using both feet to strike the same target.

**Do palmok** An assisted forearm block.

**Doo sankarak chireugi** Two-finger strike to the eyes.

**Dora** Turn. Instruction given by instructor to get class to make the turn when required.

**Doro chagi** Deflecting block using the foot against low attacks.

**Dosan** Pattern consisting of twenty-four movements.

**Dung sonkal** Reverse knife-hand or ridge hand block.

**Dung sonmok** Block using the wrist.

**Duro marki** A scoop block used for getting underneath kicking attacks to unbalance and throw the attacker.

**Dwi chagi** General term for back kicks.

**Dwichook** The bottom of the heel.

**Dwikoomchi** The back of the heel below where it joins the Achilles tendon.

**Dwiro chigi** Elbow strike to the rear.

**Dwitcha busigi** Back snap kick.

**Dwitcha jireugi** Back thrust kick.

**Dwit koaseogi** A cross-footed stance.

**Dwitkoobi** Back stance with 90 per cent of the weight on the rear foot which is pointing to the side at 90 degrees to the front foot.

**Eolgool** The face.

**Eolgool maki** Face block.

**Eotgeoreo makki** 'X'-block using the inside edges of both wrists as a trap to block kicks or punches.

**Eui am** Pattern comprising forty-five movements.

**Fugul** A back stance with 70 per cent of the weight on the rear leg.

**Gawison keut** A two-finger strike.

**Gi** Internal energy or life force, known as *chi* in Chinese and *ki* in Japanese.

**Golcho chagi** Hooking kick to the opponent's knee or elbow joint.

**Golcho makgi** Hooking block used to trap the opponent's attacking technique.

**Gomson** Curled hand.

**Gong gyuk** Attack.

**Gong gyuk gi** Attacking techniques.

**Gooleo chagi** Flying front kick.

**Goro chagi** Sweeping kick.

**Goyanghee sogi** Tiger stance.

**Gujari dolgi** The turn, ready to meet an attacker.

**Gungul sogi** Walking stance.

**Gup** Proficiency grades below the level of black belt.

**Haktari seogi** Crane stance. (Also written as **Hanbal sogi**.)

**Han mu kwan** School of Korean martial arts.

**Han songarak chirugi** One-finger strike, used to attack the eyes or the throat.

**Hansoo** A pattern consisting of twenty-seven movements.

**Hapkido** Korean martial art which emphasises the combination of strikes, kicks and throws with joint lock techniques.

**Hardan**   The part of the body below the belt.

**Hardan kyocha**   Downward 'X'-block.

**Hardan marki**   Downward block.

**Hauri**   Hip.

**Hechyo makki**   Double outward forearm block.

**Himm**   Force or power.

**Ho goo**   Protective equipment worn while sparring.

**Hohoop**   Breathing.

**Hohup chojul**   Breath control as a method of harnessing energy and prolonging endurance.

**Hooryo chagi**   A turning kick which is not pulled back if it does not hit the target but carries through as a preparatory step for the next technique.

**Hosin sul**   Techniques of self-defence.

**Hullyo marki**   Block using the arms which breaks the attacker's balance.

**Hwa-rang**   Ancient Korean knightly order, literally 'The flowering youth'.

**Hwa-rang do**   The way of the Hwa-rang, their ethical system and fighting techniques.

**Hyung**   Another word for poomse or pattern, the formal series of movements and techniques.

**Ilbo daeryon**   One-step sparring.

**Ill**   First.

**Illgup**   First class, descriptive of standard achieved in grading.

**Illyo**   Oneness, a pattern consisting of twenty-seven movements.

**Inji choomuk**   Curled hand which strikes with the middle knuckles.

**Jaejeunbal**   Evasive footwork, employed to dodge kicks and punches.

**Jeja**   Student.

**Ji do Kwan**   Korean school of martial arts.

**Jip joong**   Concentration.

**Jiptung**   Synchronising the internal and external via breathing discipline.

**Jireugi**   General term for striking.

**Jirumyo chagi**   Kick and punch combination performed while airborne.

**Jitae**   A pattern consisting of twenty-eight moves. Jitae means 'earth'.

**Jokdo**   The edge of the foot.

**Jokgi**   Foot techniques.

**Jokgi daeryon**   Pre-set sparring involving foot techniques.

**Joochoomseogi**   A high straddle stance.

**Joomeok**   Fist.

**Junbi**   Ready.

**Junbi sogi**   Ready stance.

**Kakup**   Rank

**Keumgang**   A pattern consisting of twenty-seven moves. Keumgang means 'diamond'.

**Keupso chirigi**   Art of striking the vital points of the body.

**Kihap**   Shout. Often used to add abdominal force to breaking techniques or while fighting in contest.

**Kima sogi**   Horse riding stance.

**Kup**   Grades below first Dan.

**Kupso**   The vital points of the body.

**Kwon bop**   Chinese system of unarmed combat adopted in Korea.

**Kyocha marki**   Cross block.

**Kyopka**   Breaking techniques. (Also written Kyupka.)

**Kyungye**   Bow. Instruction given by teacher during class.

**Makgi**   General term for blocking techniques.

**Mikeureumbal**   Moving the body by shifting both feet.

**Mikulgi**   Sliding movement.

**Miro makgi**   Pushing block. Uses both forearms to barge an opponent off balance.

**Mit choomuk**   Hammer fist. A strike where the bottom of the fist is used instead of the knuckles.

**Mao sogi**  Basic feet-together stance.
**Modeumbal**  Drawing the feet together.
**Modeumbal chagi**  Flying kick where both feet strike the same target.
**Mojoochoom**  Variant of straddle stance with one foot slightly forwards.
**Mokpyo**  Target areas on head or body.
**Mom**  The body.
**Momchau makgi**  A strengthened block using both forearms.
**Momdollyo chagi**  The spinning back kick.
**Momtong**  The trunk or torso.
**Momtong an maki**  Mid-section block where the blocking arm is the same as the forward leg, e.g. right leg, right arm.
**Moo duk kwan**  Korean school of martial arts.
**Moon moo**  Pattern.
**Mooreup**  The knee.
**Moseogi**  A stance where one foot is in front of the other.
**Myung chi**  The solar plexus.

**Nachugi**  Ducking technique for avoiding blows.
**Naeryo chigi**  Downward punch.
**Naeryo jiriugi**  Downward thrust.
**Naeryo marki**  Downward block.
**Najunde**  The lower part of the body; below the belt.
**Narani sogi**  A ready stance used prior to practice.
**Niunja sogi**  L-shaped stance.
**Nopunde**  The upper body including the head.
**Nopunde makgi**  High block.

**Olly o chigi**  An elbow strike delivered in an upwards direction.
**Omgyo didigi**  Covering a large gap by stepping.

**Omgyo mikulgi**  Covering ground by a sliding motion of the feet.
**Orun**  Right.

**Pachigi**  Korean martial art which makes considerable use of head-butts.
**Palgwe**  A series of patterns derived from the eight trigrams of the *I'Ching*.
**Palkoop**  Elbow.
**Palkoop chigi**  Elbow strike.
**Palmok**  Forearm or wrist.
**Phihagi**  Evasive footwork.
**Poomse**  Patterns or forms.
**Pyonson keut**  Spear hand, a strike utilising the tips of the extended fingers.
**Pyonson keut eopeochiriugi**  Twin horizontal spear hand thrust.
**Pyonson keut sewochireogi**  Vertical spear hand thrust to the solar plexus region.
**Pyugi**  Stretching.

**Sabom**  Teacher or instructor.
**Sambo daeryon**  Three-step sparring.
**Sandan marki**  The upward block.
**Sangdan**  The face and head area.
**Sangdan kyocha marki**  'X'-block against attack to face.
**Sasun sogi**  Diagonal stance.
**Sewo chiriugi**  Vertical punch.
**Shejak**  Begin.
**Shibum**  Demonstration.
**Shihap**  Contest, bout or match.
**Simsa**  Grading examination.
**Sogi**  Stance.
**Sokdo**  Speed.
**Sokim**  Feint.
**Sonbadak**  Palm.
**Sondung**  Back fist.
**Songdung mok marki**  Bent wrist block.
**Sonnal**  Knife-hand. (Also written **Sonkal**.)

**Sonnal deung**  Reverse knife-hand.
**Sonnal marki**  Knife block.
**Soobak**  Korean fighting system dating from the twelfth century
**Sudo**  Knife-hand.

**Taebaek**  A pattern consisting of twenty-six moves.
**Taegeuk**  A series of eight fundamental patterns.
**Taekwondo**  The way of fist and foot, can also be translated 'To smash with fist or foot'. The most popular of the eclectic Korean fighting arts.
**Taesudo**  Original name given to tae-kwondo.
**Tang soo do**  The art of the Chinese hand. A Korean fighting system strongly influenced by Japanese karate.

**Twichibo chiriugi**  A punch delivered with the palm upwards, such as an upper-cut and some hooks.

**Yaksok daeryon**  Pre-arranged sparring.
**Yeebo daeryon**  Two-step sparring.
**Yeop chagi**  The side-kick.
**Yeop makki**  Side block.
**Yeopeurochigi**  Horizontal elbow strike.
**Yichoong chagi**  Double kick.
**Yichoong Marki**  Double block.
**Yikwon**  Back fist.
**Yok sudo**  Reverse knife-hand.
**Yon sok**  Combination.
**Yop jireugi**  Side punch.
**Yop chagi**  Side kick.
**Yop Marki**  Side block.
**Yu sin**  A pattern composed of sixty-eight movements.

# Useful Addresses

The Taekwondo Association of Great Britain
7 Lime Avenue
Lillington
Leamington Spa
Warwickshire CV32 7DE

The British Taekwondo Federation
91 Vine Street
Darlington
County Durham DL3 6HP

The United Kingdom Taekwondo Association
Head Office, Suite 2
100 The Centre
Feltham
Middlesex TW13 4BN

United Kingdom Choi Kwang Do Federation
'Pil Sung'
Mornington Road
Ashford
Middlesex TW15 1NW

Graham Rance
The Secretary
The British Taekwondo Board of Control
14 Hedgeside
Potten End
Berkhamstead
Hertfordshire HP4 2RE

# Index

# Other Martial Arts Books Published By The Crowood Press

* Armlocks — Neil Adams

Contest Judo — Roy Inman with Nicolas Soames

Karate – The Skills of the Game — Vic Charles

Judo Champion — Karen Briggs

Judo for Women — Roy Inman with Nicolas Soames

Judo – Skills and Techniques — Tony Reay

Practical Women's Judo — Roy Inman with Nicolas Soames

* Tomoe-nage — Katsuhiko Kashiwazaki

* Ippon Books